GOD IN THE HEART OF THINGS

Published to honor the thought and labors of the Very Reverend Hughell E. W. Fosbroke, D.D., S.T.D., LL.D., late Dean of The General Seminary, New York City, Honorary Canon of the Cathedral Church of St. John the Divine, and Trustee of The Seabury Press.

EDWARD FRENCH, *Editor*

GOD
IN THE HEART
OF THINGS

by Hughell E. W. Fosbroke

 With an introductory memoir by
Stephen F. Bayne, Jr.

GREENWICH · CONNECTICUT · 1962

❧ Publisher's Note

The papers and addresses of Dean Fosbroke which are gathered here have been chosen because they convey in a representative way the sensitivity and sweep of the Dean's thought. Everyone who knew the Dean or had the opportunity to hear him recognized the eloquence with which he spoke, as well as the penetration and insight which characterized his treatment of the subject at hand. But, above all, they recognized the Dean's God-centeredness. And these selected papers are essentially about that one Person—"the God who has been at work bringing men to a truer appreciation of life's splendor."

The occasion of the various papers will be of interest to many readers. "God and His Creation" was originally a series of three lectures given in the early 40's to the Ministerial Association of New York City. The substance of these lectures were used later in other forms at the General Seminary. The last dozen or so pages here are the concluding lecture of a course, "God as Revealed in the Old Testament"; this concluding lecture the Dean was unable to deliver, but dictated so that copies might be distributed among his students.

The section, "The Ministry and Theological Education," includes "The One Foundation," the sermon preached by the Dean on the occasion of his installation in the deanship of the General Seminary on February 5, 1917. The other two essays in the section bore nothing indicating the occasion for which they were composed.

"Prophecy in Revelation" were the Reinicker Lectures, delivered at the Virginia Seminary in January, 1937; they also formed the basis of the Dean's article on Prophecy in the *Interpreter's Bible*. Both papers included in the section, "The Church" appeared some years ago in *The Living Church*.

All the excerpts in the section, Obiter Dicta, are from papers originally prepared in the early 30's to be read before an informal reading circle composed of faculty members from General Seminary and Union Seminary in New York City.

Acknowledgment must be made of the gracious encouragement of Miss Esther Fosbroke, the late Dean's daughter; the generous labors of the Rev. Edward French; and the encouragement and guidance given by the late Dean's friends and colleagues at the General Seminary: the Rt. Rev. Stephen F. Bayne, Jr., the Very Rev. Cuthbert A. Simpson, and the Rev. Professors W. Norman Pittenger and Harvey H. Guthrie, Jr. A debt is also owed to Mrs. Dorothy Fitzgerald for her devoted efforts with the manuscript, and to the Rev. R. W. Corney, who gave help with the proofreading.

❧ Contents

❧ Hughell E. W. Fosbroke:
A Memoir

This book brings together some important examples of the thought of Hughell Fosbroke. It was characteristic of him—inordinately shy and profoundly humble—that almost never did he permit himself to be published, much less to shape any of his immense, acute, and scholarly wisdom for publication. He wrote prodigiously, but only rarely to be read. Most of his writing was for his eyes alone (and for the ears of his students, subsequently). Few of us who heard him lecture suspected the meticulous care with which his lectures were prepared, or the way in which, year after year, they were rewritten, rephrased, in tireless search for the exact word, the balanced and powerful and communicating sentence. But we were not to be blamed for this. He spoke with such intensity that it was hard to imagine how he had worked over what he was to say. And if we grumbled because we might not read his thought, a snort, half-derisive, half-modest, was usually our only answer.

I suspect that there were many roots of this reticence. In part, he was burdened with the care of a large academic family, at a major turning point in its history. His thirty years at the General Theological Seminary (1917-1947), spanned two world wars and the perplexing time of the Depression. Even more, it was his vocation to lead the Seminary into a new idea of itself and a new phase of its ministry; and this profound rebirth cost untold hours of his energy and interest. In part, too, he had so sensitive and deep a respect for the true standards of scholarship that he found it impossible to accept the estimate of his own scholarly work which others freely gave. Even more, his restless mind made it distasteful for him to crystallize attitudes or commit himself to positions or details of exegesis, such as publication requires. All this, coupled with his natural shyness, doubtless nourished his reluctance to write for publication.

At all events, it will be most gratifying to many that Mr. French has brought together these writings. They are not fragments; they are not the left-over "remains" of a voluminous writer; they are vivid passages—lectures, reviews, essays and the like—which are of very considerable intrinsic worth as well as moving reminders to all who had the privilege of being the students of an extraordinary teacher.

As teacher, indeed, will and should he be remembered. Yet this is in itself curious, for teaching was by no means his only role during a long life. For that matter, in many ways the greatest gift he made to the American Church was the reordering of the life of the General Seminary itself. It is not only pride which prompts me to say that "The General" plays a major part in the life of the American Church. As the oldest and largest of the Church's seminaries, and the only one established and controlled by the Church as a whole, through the General Convention, it cannot help but be a bellwether of theological education in the Episcopal Church. And it fell to Dean Fosbroke to be not only the architect but as well the builder of the new form of theological education which came into being in Chelsea Square during the first decade of his administration.

The tutorial system was the most radical element in this new form, I suppose, for it meant that the teaching community was more than doubled, and the dynamics of the teaching process were profoundly changed. But perhaps of even greater consequence was the galaxy of teachers he brought to General. In my own time, doubtless a golden age, Burton Scott Easton, Frank Gavin, Leonard Hodgson, and Marshall Bowyer Stewart held the primary chairs, and each of them had come to Chelsea Square because of the leadership of the Dean. It was an incomparable company; and it was Dean Fosbroke who had imagined it and brought it together—more, who led it and gave it coherence and was himself the focus around which it gathered.

This was a major role, in truth, this administrative leadership he gave during those years when, to my mind, the Seminary was really coming of age. But he played a part in the life of the American Church in other ways, too. His reports to the General Convention, for example, were often remarkable documents, and always thought-provoking, and sometimes nettlesome; and always, while he spoke with great respect, he spoke as one who discerned the set of the tide as few could do. And what should be said of still another role— that of the thoughtful and tireless adviser to so many who turned to him? I know of others who, like myself, learned to bring all our root decisions to him, sure of understanding, sure of affectionate helpfulness, sure of a diamond judgment that cut deep and clean. Then, too, there was the incredible range of his reading, informing an eager, critical mind, so that even his table talk became a lesson, sometimes acid, sometimes prophetic, in the cultural history through which we were living.

But in all these phases of his life and ministry, he remained pre-eminently the teacher. That is why I say it is as teacher that he will and should be remembered. It is certainly so with me. I had the privilege of knowing him for nearly thirty years, first while I was a student and then a tutor, then as a friend and my counsellor in increasing warmth and confidence until his death. It was not always easy to know him, for he could be a forbidding disciplinarian. Being a New York boy myself, and inclined to fit my theological studies into a somewhat luxuriant extra-curricular life, there was a time or two when my attention needed to be recalled to some of the central aspects of seminary life; and it was done, and not uncertainly. And there were moments in later days, when I was a fellow and tutor, which I still remember with a twinge. The Dean had no mercy on cant, on the party line or the party jargon, whatever it was; and there were not many of us "small fry" at the high table who did not wince occasionally, when he would elect to wither us for some silly comment or other.

Yet how unimportant these painful moments seem, as I look back on them and remember the thousand and one other times when his restless, exacting, penetrating love for us was so clear. Once at a particularly difficult meeting of the General Convention, I came in to the hotel coffee shop late at night, bruised and bewildered by a debate which seemed to be completely untrue to the Church I thought I had known, and torn by doubts as to whether there was any unity in the Church at all. Nobody else was at the counter except the Dean, sipping his cup of chocolate and reading some periodical or other. And how I wept on his shoulder! And how he lifted my spirits and restored my perspective; and he did this not by smooth words, but by raising the whole controversy to the level where it should be—where God's judgment and God's love could play on it and bring order into it. His experience played a part in it, of course, for there were not many in the Church who had seen more than he had, and none who understood it better. But the greater thing was that he never "thought small" of the Church. He always saw it in the grandeur of its true nature as Israel—judging, judged, witnessing, suffering, existing, proclaiming, rejoicing. He taught this, to every one of us.

Mostly, of course, he taught it in his lectures, those unforgettable summits when the greatness of the God of Israel first became dimly clear to us. Long afterwards I learned how meticulously he prepared them. At the time, there seemed no structure to them at all—he simply became Hosea, became Amos; and for two hours he held such worldlings as myself enthralled with the vision of what the Old Testament was about. To this day I cannot read the Song of Deborah, or hear Hosea, "When Israel was a child, then I loved him, and called my son out of Egypt," or remembered Jeremiah, "Say not, I am a child," without hearing him, and remembering the almost infinite recesses of meaning which he opened to us in those far off days.

He was a teacher, par excellence. I repeat this, with added weight, because of the brilliant company of teachers with which he had surrounded himself. He did not seek conformity in his colleagues; he did not understand the Seminary's vocation as that of preserving inherited faith; he had no interest in making it a safe place for pious young men. Indeed, he shared quite deeply the traditional Anglican suspicion of the "seminarist mind," and shared to the full the humane protest against the isolation of theological study from other studies. Inescapably there were clear and sometimes painful tensions to be met, within the seminary community, precisely because of the extraordinary variety of the men who shared academic leadership with him. It was never his way to urge the happy ending, academically. If there was uncomfortable tension, say, between Easton's uncompromising standards of criticism and Stewart's gently and broadly classical unities, the tension had to be faced. Faced it was, indeed, and contained within the worshipping community, as such strain must ever be, if the Church is to be the Church. But the differences, the paradoxes, the mental pains must not be softened. Therefore, inescapably, the excitement of learning was sometimes fantastically high, and the allegiance of the learners correspondingly personal and devoted. Yet he seemed always at one with all the others; he was the unity of the seminary, more often than not; and in this was perhaps the highest proof of his teaching skill.

I cannot, even now, write coolly and dispassionately about him, any more than I could of any of the others of that astonishing company. Yet I want to set out something more than merely personal reminiscences, to try to express my sense of Hughell Fosbroke's unique place in the American Church. Perhaps I can indicate that sense by making an excursion into some broad thoughts about American theological education in general.

In my time as a student—to a large extent even now—theological education in the Episcopal Church could not be understood apart from England and the Church of England. This is partly a matter of textbooks. The basic library of an American theological student in my day was much like that of his British counterpart. The field within which our philosophical argument proceeded was established principally by British teachers—Alexander, Bosanquet, Bradley, Pringle-Pattison, Taylor, Webb. Gore and Temple were the giants, of course; but the twin volumes of Essays—*Catholic and Critical* and *On the Trinity and Incarnation*—introduced us to other names. Hoskyns, Rawlinson, Streeter, Thornton, were major figures in Biblical studies. *Liturgy and Worship,* and Procter and Frere, were staples in our beginning liturgical diet. Kirk was our unique tutor in moral theology. Indeed, the list is long; and among my own books, to this day, the marks of that dependence on the steady flow of British scholarship are clear.

This was not at all a matter of some supposed Anglophilia on the part of Episcopalians. We read plenty of other books (perhaps here more fully than our British counterparts)—the criticism of my day was often dominated by the Germans. There were exciting new currents flowing from Scandinavia. De la Taille and Von Hildebrand were stirring deeper thoughts about liturgy. And the more mysterious giants—Barth, Brunner, Tillich—loomed on the horizon. And to that list must be added the American scholars—Bacon, Hocking, the two Niebuhrs, Scott. No, it was not a provincial Anglophilia, at all. The fact was that the Church of England, alone among the Anglican Churches, was able to devote so great a measure of its strength to scholarly work. Its ancient endowments were not an unmixed blessing; but they did serve to set creative minds free for the slow work of learning and thinking and writing, to a degree unparalleled anywhere else. I often think of the vivid and intense young minds I knew and taught, and wonder at the necessity which so often directed them into the exacting and sometimes dulling routine of the parish ministry—wonder at it not because there is any nobler impulse than that which brings a priest to a parish, but because it is such wretched economy in the life of the Church to find no way to put such brains to work in the seed beds of theology.

I am not negligent of the scholarship of the Episcopal Church, in such measure as there was. Du Bose, unhappily, was a neglected prophet in my generation, though William Sanday called him "the wisest Anglican writer . . . on both sides of the Atlantic." But F. J. Hall, that unique Anglican encyclopedist, lived in vivid memory in the General; Burton Easton doubtless holds the pre-eminent place among Anglican scholars in his massive introduction of form-criticism; Frank Gavin, had it not been for his untimely death, would surely have fulfilled the immense variety of his knowledge and his brilliant insights; Paul More was a powerful and disconcerting scholar, who probably understood the Anglican genius and tradition more completely than anyone of his time. I speak of them because they played so great a part in my own education. As well, let them be witnesses to the productive scholarship which was then beginning to bear its generous harvest.

But the fact still remains that our books were British books in largest measure. In turn, this meant that there was a profound British cast and tradition of mind, in our theological education. We were sometimes more familiar with British intellectual and spiritual frontiers than we were with our own, and were equally predisposed to the British solutions. This could have been, and often was, a dangerous familiarity indeed. Many of us, in our younger days, at any rate, ran the constant risk of becoming diluted Englishmen, instead of what we should have been. And here too, Anglophilia was a persistent problem. It was so easy to fall in love with the spirit of an Oxford common room or a London slum parish, and so be blinded to the American counterparts within which it was to be our vocation to minister. But there was a positive side to it, for it meant that the singular Anglican turn of mind, that humane, historical sense which is so bright a star in the Anglican constellation, was being transplanted; and it was and is one of the better British exports. It needs to become indigenous, this spirit. But when it does, as has so often happened in American and Commonwealth history, the result is a nourishing and vigorous blend of old and new which has been of the greatest significance in the development of our civilization.

There are moments, now, when it seems to me that I understand the Anglican genius far better than those who live in its native land. Perhaps this ought not be surprising, for it is often true that the stranger sees us better than we see ourselves. But I would trace it to more than that. As far as it is true it is so because an Amercian Anglican student had a double intellectual task—both to learn within a largely British setting and tradition, and then to interpret and convert this knowledge into another setting. But be that as it may, the fact was, once again, that theological education in the American Church could not be understood apart from theological education in the Church of England.

A third illustration comes to mind—the extraordinary influence of the institutions of the Church of England on its daughter churches. The American Church is something of a maverick in the Anglican family. Because we were the first province to come into independent life outside the British Isles, and also because of the political history involved, the Episcopal Church was, of necessity, far more free in improvising and experimenting than its younger sisters often were. Not all the improvising was of permanent value; some of it doubtless was misleading and untrue; but for the most part I should feel thankful for it, and feel that it has introduced valuable new ideas and practices into the Anglican bloodstream. Yet despite all this, it is perfectly clear that, as our Prayer Book's Preface says, "This Church is far from intending to depart from the Church of England in any essential point of doctrine, discipline, or worship; or further than local circumstances require."

Practically, this meant that the ordinand of my day was trained against the background of a settled, national church, living its life within the parochial system. If he happened, as I did, to be a child of the Eastern seaboard, it was easier for him to understand and accept that background, for it was not radically different from what he himself had known. To the Western American, it must have been more of an adventure. But however this might be, we were taught to think of our ministry as that of the Church, not of a sect. The "parish" was still more a matter of geography than sociology to us. The notion of the whole responsibility of the Church to its community was deep in us. The religious life of our society seemed part and parcel of its total life, to us. All this was "English"; and I think it was good.

Despite the irrelevances of the parochial system to a polycultural society like America, it is still good for us in the clergy to act like ministers of the Church of the land rather than denominational wizards. Of course, the parochial system is an anachronism; it is so in England, too; but as long as it survives in our bones, it is possible to live in a society composed of many religious minorities and still keep the depth and greatness of the sense of a responsible national Church.

Of course there are dangers—and here Anglophilia is at its worst. The senseless transplanting into America, as into other parts of the world, of British ecclesiastical eccentricities is a risk all of us run; and, alas, the risk to our mission is far graver than to our own good sense. But the good gifts are worth the risk, I think. So I was led to feel, at any rate, in my theological education.

I have mentioned three aspects of the dependence of theological education in the Episcopal Church on that of the Church of England. In the thirty years since my own days at Chelsea Square, much has changed. "Dependence" now is becoming "inter-dependence," a far healthier relationship between two sister churches and nations. American scholarship now is far more mature, and far more self-confident. The American seminary has lessons to teach as well as learn. Theological education in the American Church, for example, has now a rich tradition of intelligent experimentation in pastoral theology which I wish might be widely imitated elsewhere in our Anglican family. So again is there an excitement about teaching, in a sizable and balanced community of scholars, which is impossible to achieve in the smaller groups, often dominated by one teacher, still characteristic of most Anglican provinces. Still another example might well be found in the seriousness with which critical, historical Biblical study is undertaken in the American seminary.

Much indeed has changed. But the fact remains still that the life of the Episcopal Church is inextricably interwoven with that of the Church of England, particularly our intellectual life. Far from regretting this, I rejoice in it, and long to see the time when it will also be inextricably interwoven with that of every other Anglican Church, perhaps most of all, with that of our neighbors to the North. What is utterly essential, if this interdependence is to bear its fruit, is that the interpreters of it shall be men who move loftily and freely in both worlds. We do not want transplanted Englishmen trying to convert American theological students to a "Better Mind," nor will Anglican unity be served by brash Americans who see an English village simply as a retarded American suburb. The interpreter must be one who can move freely among cultures, who without trying to abandon his own roots (which he could not do in any case) yet can discern humanity and truth in their sometimes terrifying, and always exalting, unities, in and through mankind's divided traditions.

Such an interpreter was Hughell Fosbroke, a child of the Church of England, who yet gave to the American Church unparalleled understanding of its own vocation within its own national culture. It was the good fortune of more than 1500 priests of the Episcopal Church to share the life of the General Seminary during his years as Dean. Forty-five of those students became bishops—forty-one of them bishops of the Anglican Communion. There are not many men in the history of the Episcopal Church who have played any larger part in the life of the clergy of that Church than did he. But it is not the numbers that matter; what matters is the depth of understanding which was communicated to them. The more I think about it, the more thankful I am for the five years I spent in Chelsea Square, as the beneficiary of just such teaching as these following pages contain.

STEPHEN F. BAYNE, JR.

GOD AND HIS CREATION

⮞ God and His Creation

"Thus saith the high and lofty One that inhabiteth eternity, whose name is Holy; I dwell in the high and lofty place, with him also that is of a contrite and humble spirit, to revive the spirit of the humble, and to revive the heart of the contrite ones."—Is. 57:15

This is the utterance of one who is keenly aware of the immediacy of the relationship of God to his own life. Sadly conscious of sin and with a sense of hopeless failure, he has found himself lifted out of the slough of despond, and given new courage to go forward, by the act of God drawing him into union with himself. But what, above all, excited his wondering awe is that this gracious intimacy is that of the God of all power and might, the high and holy One whose name is Holy—in the language of today, the transcendent God.

It is, of course, one of the great services of the movement in theology first associated with the name of Karl Barth, but now broadened into what is known as neo-orthodoxy, that it has in large measure restored a gravely needed emphasis on the primary significance of the divine transcendence. In fact, this has become one of the key words in any discussion of religion. Where the theologian of an older day spoke of the supernatural, neo-orthodoxy uses the word "transcendent" to express the qualitative distinction between God and man.

Phrases such as "the wholly Other," "the unknown God," "the hidden God," serve as the needed reminder that the ultimate reality of the Divine Being is infinitely beyond our categories of thought and explanation. And, at its best, neoorthodoxy provides the necessary qualification of these phrases by insisting that the same wholly other, unknown, hidden God does indeed give to those who will receive it such knowledge of himself as the limitations of finite human understanding will allow. Only it may be asked whether the revelation given in the long discipline of Israel's history does not reflect a far more pervasive implication of God's giving of himself in human life than much of the modern emphasis on transcendence would appear to recognize. For Christian faith it is, indeed, in the life and death and rising again of Jesus Christ that God has most fully declared himself but in all this as bringing into closer and more pervasive saving relationship to this world of ours the sovereign power, the absolute righteousness, the holy love of the dynamic personal being of the God who had revealed himself in every aspect of the history of this chosen people, chosen to be the vehicle of that revelation.

It was the break through of a new awareness of the divine transcendence upon a group of nomad tribes that marked the beginning of Israel's knowledge of Yahweh, for significantly enough he made himself known to them in just those aspects of nature which seem to deny the meaning and the worth of human life. He was the God of storm. Mt. Sinai was the especial scene of his manifestation of power. The description of that mountain in Exodus (19:18), "smoke ascending as the smoke of a furnace while the whole mount quaked greatly," would appear to preserve the memory of volcanic eruption as marking the presence of Israel's God. Yahweh was a great awe-inspiring deity whose power was revealed in destroying violence, the death-dealing God of storm whose might declared itself in the tempest that swept resistlessly over the face of the earth, whose voice could be heard in the thunder, whose arm was laid bare in the blinding lightning flash. Or again, the explosive upheaval of fire from the bowels of the earth with the devastating lava flow was a characteristic manifestation of the divine energy. Such was the God of Israel as a nature God. And throughout Israel's history the sense of the immeasurable might and mysterious majesty of God, dwarfing human effort and achievement to insignificance, at times sweeping everything away in the overwhelming flow of destroying energy, found every now and again vivid expression. Here is the prophet Isaiah speaking of the coming of the day of the Lord:

For there shall be a day of Yahweh of hosts upon all that is proud and haughty, and upon all that is lifted up; and it shall be brought low; and upon all the cedars of Lebanon, that are high and lifted up, and upon all the oaks of Bashan, and upon all the high mountains, and upon all the hills that are lifted up, and upon every lofty tower, and upon every fortified wall, and upon all the ships of Tarshish, and upon all pleasant imagery. And the loftiness of man shall be bowed down, and the haughtiness of men shall be brought low; and Yahweh alone shall be exalted in that day. And the idols shall utterly pass away. And men shall go into the caves of the rocks, and into the holes of the earth, from before the terror of Yahweh, and from the glory of his majesty, when he ariseth to shake mightily the earth. (2:12-19)

Or again, a passage in the book of the Prophet Nahun:

The Lord hath his way in the whirlwind and in the storm, and the clouds are the dust of his feet. Who can stand before his indignation and who can abide in the fierceness of his anger? His fury is poured out like fire and the rocks are thrown down by him. (1:3, 6)

Or once more hear the psalmist:

O come hither and behold the works of the Lord.
What destruction he hath brought upon the earth.

And as we note the irony with which he goes on to say,

He maketh wars to cease in all the world,
He breaketh the bow and knappeth the spear
asunder, and burneth the chariots in the fire (46:8-9).

we learn that man's inherent power of destroying violence as manifest in war is as nothing before the might and majesty of the living God. And, no doubt, he would have been quite ready to maintain this even if told of the atom bomb.

But Israel's God was not only the God of storm and earthquake; he exercised his power also within the life of man. He was the God of war. In the great triumphal ode known as the Song of Deborah, the oldest extant monument of Hebrew literature, Yahweh is represented as fighting not only for men but through men. In the wild frenzy of the conflict, in the overmastering impulses that carried a band of warriors on a death-defying charge, the divine energy made itself felt. As the storm raged, the passion in their hearts answered to the fury of the elements and they hurled themselves upon the foe in an onslaught that carried all before it. The driving power of Israel's religion can be understood only as this experience of demonic energy, finding expression in nature and in human hearts, is given recognition.

For it is, of course, in terms of experience rather than of theology that any religion must ultimately be considered. Israel did not begin by saying "Our God is both God of storm and God of war." These phrases were the result of the effort to formulate the meaning of what had happened to them. It would appear that for the nomad tribes there had been times when in the presence of the dread manifestation of destroying power in storm or earthquake or volcanic eruption the self-regarding instinct to tremble for their own safety gave place to awe-struck wonder at the splendor of the manifestation of power. Then, with self forgotten, they found themselves drawn into union with a force infinitely greater than themselves. Therefore, shrinking terror was replaced by a strange exaltation which carried with it a sense of heightened capacity, an exhilaration of the whole being. In the total surrender to One who claimed them wholly for his own purpose, there was the beginning of a new realization of what is meant to be drawn into relationship to a transcendent God, possessed of incalculable power, unpredictable in its movement and absolutely beyond anything like human control.

Lest you should be tempted to think that this experience belongs only to a far-off barbarous time, let me call to witness a twentieth-century writer, the distinguished Shakespearian scholar A. C. Bradley. In his *Oxford Lectures on Poetry* he tries to convey what is to be found in the experience of the sublime. There are, he says, two equally necessary phases, a negative and a positive, a sense of an overwhelming greatness which for a moment checks, baffles, subdues, even repels us or makes us feel our littleness, and then, at a second stage, forces its way into the imagination and emotion, uplifting them to its own dimensions. We burst our own limits, go out to the sublime thing, identify ourselves ideally with it and share its immense greatness—we rise into union with the law which imposes on us an unconditional demand or with the infinite source and end of our spiritual life.

Many of you will doubtless see at once that what we are thinking of is, to use the term that Rudolph Otto has made familiar, the "numinous," the *mysterium tremendum,* the mystery that makes us shudder while at the same time it is *fascinans,* possessed of a strange power to break in upon us and draw us into union with itself. Otto's book *The Idea of the Holy* has become a classic, and theological scholarship is indebted beyond all telling to his masterly exposition. If one may dare to criticize so great a work, it would be to suggest that in his necessary preoccupation with the extraordinary movements of experience the writer does not sufficiently insist on the pervasive character of the numinous as it can be discerned in the ordinary experience of everyday life. Tennyson's flower in the crannied wall is a case in point. The word *tremendum* (that which makes one shudder) has its significant place in the history of religion, but in face of the mystery of life there are also more ordinary feelings of perhaps less pronounced character which must be taken into account. And so I want to dwell briefly on the part that the sense of bafflement, of being checked, of inadequacy in the presence of the demands that life makes upon us, plays in preparing the way for that *breaking in* upon us of power from on high that we know as the grace of God in revelation, redemption, and sanctification. It may help if I venture an illustration from another phase of interest. In his book *Aesthetics and History* Bernard Berenson, perhaps the greatest of modern art critics, recounts the following experience.

For years I had been inquiring, excavating, dredging my inner self and searching in my conscious experience for a satisfying test [of beauty]. I needed a test to apply to the artifacts [objects of art] that I thought I admired but could not hypnotize or habituate myself to enjoy with complete abandon. . . . Then one morning, as I was gazing at the leafy scrolls carved on the door jambs of S. Pietro outside Spoleto, suddenly stem, tendrils and foliage became alive and, in becoming alive, made me feel as if I had emerged into the light after long groping in the darkness of an initiation. I felt as one illumined and beheld a world where every outline, every edge and every surface was in a *living* relation to me and not as hitherto in a merely cognitive one. Since that morning nothing visible has been indifferent or even dull. Everywhere I feel the ideated pulsation of vitality . . .

You will, I am sure, admit that this can be called an experience of conversion, and indeed the writer describes it as in essence a mystical experience. Let us note the steps that led up to it. There is the unsparing effort, what he calls the inquiring, excavating, dredging of his inner self, but all this dictated by a consuming passion for the Other than himself Beauty to which he may give complete abandon because it claims him for its own, Beauty so transcendent that the quest for it leaves him hopelessly baffled. At last he realizes that underlying his effort as shown by the search for a test, a definition, is the unconscious desire to bring beauty within his grasp. It is only when the self has by this failure of its own intensive effort been reduced as it were to the vanishing point in an overwhelming sense of its own insignificance that its passionate reverence for beauty opens the way to the realization that it is just there existing in its own magnificent right, demanding not explanation but the homage of adoring love, not something that can be taken into possession, formulated and catalogued, but that which breaking through takes possession of one's whole being, claims one for its own and determines one's whole outlook upon life so that nothing visible is thenceforth indifferent, but everywhere is vitality, energy, radiance.

Parallel to this in striking degree is the approach to reality which Dr. Paul Tillich describes in a monograph written some years ago, entitled *Justification and Doubt*. In it he gives a brilliant account of the way in which through the centuries the discipline of monasticism and the sacrament of Penance had brought sensitive souls to the realization of the moral law as exacting an absolute and total obedience of one's whole being and, consequently, of the hopelessness of obtaining righteousness before God by one's own effort. It was upon the sense of their own helpless inadequacy, baffled by the intensity of their longing for that deliverance from their state of sinfulness which should set them in the right relationship to the all-holy God that there broke in upon them the full realization that that God was in Christ reconciling the world unto himself, that it was this saving force of the life and death of Jesus that was manifest in their very being as he was claiming them for himself, so that in response to the divine activity their whole outlook upon life could be changed as everywhere they could discern the goodness of God seeking to save that which was lost.

But since the Renaissance, Dr. Tillich tells us, there has gradually come about a change in men's questioning. Instead of seeking, in the first instance, "What need I do to be saved?" they are asking, "Is there, after all, a God who can save so that life really has a meaning and is not simply a day-to-day existence between the darkness of the womb and of the grave?" It is, I think, true that the desperate need of an answer to this question is more widely and keenly felt in a Europe in which all the horrors of war have been so disastrously felt than it is on this side of the Atlantic. But here, too, as the result of the breakdown of traditions, the overthrow of values that had always been taken for granted, and as a result also of the conviction that in some way or another the advance of critical scientific inquiry has left little room for God, there is, on the one hand, a widespread feeling that at best God is no more than an hypothesis for Christian thinking, and, on the other, a craving for that certainty about his actual existence that can alone give the assurance of an ultimate meaning for life. I am inclined to think that this feeling and this craving are more widely diffused even among the people in our pews than we are wont to think. It interested me, when talking with one of the leaders of a Parish Life Conference that the Department of Education was conducting, to learn that a statement not infrequently made by mothers ran something like this: "The thing I want above all is that my child shall learn really to believe in God." Many people, to be sure, are content with accepting authoritative pronouncement on the subject whether it be that of a church or simply that of age-long tradition, but increasingly there are great numbers of thoughtful people, both within and without our churches, who can be satisfied with nothing less than a conviction that is the result of their own fearless seeking of the truth. Theirs is the spirit that underlies all that is best in scientific inquiry, that will face all the facts, bent only on arriving at the truth. And to this quest for truth they, like those who care intensely for beauty or goodness, are willing to devote the unsparing use of all the powers that they possess. And again and again they find themselves in the end confronted only by baffling mystery. The more they wrestle with the problem of whether there is a God and life, therefore, has meaning, the more they find their doubts driving them on to despair. But it is just at that point that there should come to them realization that the truth they are seeking is so tremendous that it cannot be attained simply by their own efforts, much as these may prepare the way for it. It breaks in upon them that it is simply there, the presupposition of all their seeking. In their intense longing for it and their unsparing effort, the living energy of God himself has been at work in their lives, claiming their homage and obedience. In the words of Tillich: "The breaking through brings the certainty that the truth which the doubter seeks, the meaning of life for which despair is struggling, is not the goal but the presupposition of all doubt, even to the point of despair." I am reminded of a limerick in which, I think, it was Ronald Knox, who held up to scorn the liberals of his day:

> O God, for as much as without thee
> We are not able to doubt thee,
> O grant us thy grace
> To tell all the race
> We know nothing at all about thee.

I am not sure whether Msgr. Knox, as he is now, appreciated the full significance of the admission that the liberals knew their dependence upon God for their very doubting, or whether he was simply pointing to the inconsistency of their further affirmation that they knew nothing about the God who had thus broken in upon their lives.

Or, in more serious mood, some of the older men among us will remember a time when much was made of William James' insistence on the importance of the will to believe as offering a hopeful approach to religious conviction. Later it was realized that for those who did not bring to the desire to believe the scrupulously honest intellectual effort of the philosopher, it could easily open the way to every kind of aberration because it made man the center from which he could move in any direction he pleased. It was L. P. Jacks, the distinguished editor for many years of the *Hibbert Journal,* who pointed out that God was not so much the goal as the source of the will to believe.

To find God breaking through into life in that ardent desire for truth that can in these days involve so much of doubt and even despair, is to prepare the way for that discernment everywhere of the unceasing movement of his will that can change the whole outlook upon life.

It may seem a far cry from the group of nomad tribes of long ago, huddled in wondering awe before the mysterious power of storm and earthquake, and the earnest seeker for reality, baffled to the point of despair by the overwhelming mystery of the universe, but both alike find a meaning for life when power breaks through; and power breaks through when, looking away from self and its claims, men become aware of the constant priority of the divine activity. Indeed, that is the first and all-important note of the teaching about God in the Old Testament. In that strange experience of possession by the God of destroying energy, Israel had known itself a chosen people called into being for a particular purpose by God himself. And so there is no attempt in the Old Testament to prove the existence of God. Zophar the Naamathite takes for granted the general recognition of the folly of such effort when he puts the rhetorical question: "Canst thou by searching find out God?" (Job 11:7) God is the presupposition of all our thinking. In the words of the Psalmist, "He understandeth our thoughts long before." And so everywhere and always it is the divine activity that is to be seen unfailingly at work.

The lions roaring after their prey do seek their meat from God—and he giveth them their meat in due season. Wind and storm are seen as fulfilling his word. And the Old Testament can present human nature as it is in all its weakness and its strength without any false optimism, on the one hand, or any crippling pessimism, on the other, because the God of infinite power and untiring love is working out his purpose through the activity of human wills. That purpose may seem at times to be defeated. So, in Israel's history, the nation that he had called into being came to a pitiful end because it had sought to use God rather than be used by him, but out of the fragments a new community was brought into being that, amid all the vicissitudes of exile, could bear its testimony to the active presence of the one transcendent righteous God, knitting men together in the bonds of an abiding fellowship; and the same God is at work in his world today.

It was, as you know, through Moses' successors that there came the gradual development of the law, the Torah, which all through the centuries has played so significant a role in Judaism.

Priests and judges gave their decisions in the disputes brought before them, and there followed, as time went on, the codification of these decisions into bodies of law. As we look back upon the process, we are wont to think of these decisions as simple directives indicating the line of conduct to be followed. We overlook what it meant, that they were felt to be binding because the word of God spoke through them. For the word was not, as we who are familiar with the printed page are accustomed to think, just an inert sign. Into the spoken word went the personality of the speaker, and the word of God was regarded, as Professor Millar Burrows of Yale puts it, as "an active extension of the [divine] presence." In the decision rendered, the very righteousness of God himself was felt to be at work, intervening in the clash of human wills. That was why the law was held to be so sacred, so that today even the roll of the Torah is treated with the utmost reverence.

It is, then, on righteousness as power, the very power of God himself at work in the world, that our attention should be fastened. We are so prone to let our thinking issue in abstractions that that righteousness, for the most part, comes to be regarded as an ideal, a pattern, laid up in the heavens to which in some way human life must be brought to conform. Professor Snaith, a very able English scholar, in his book *Some Distinctive Ideas of the Old Testament,* defines righteousness as that which God himself established as the proper norm, which on that account is firm and straight, steady and immovable. The definition is right insofar as it insists on God's unfailing consistency as a note of his righteousness; but when the definition speaks of a norm as something immovable, it misses the sense of the immediacy of the divine activity, of the movement of the will of God in any particular situation, seeking to effect the divine purpose for good that may be brought out of the situation. Therein lies the primary meaning of the word. So it is that in the Old Testament, not infrequently, righteousness is found in association with the idea of salvation, especially in the positive meaning of this word as sounding the note of triumphant issue from difficult and constraining conditions. Indeed, in that same primitive poem, known as the Song of Deborah, to which I have already referred, we read, "There shall they rehearse the righteous acts of Yahweh"; and the context makes it clear that the reference is to victories that God has won for his people.

The exercise of the divine activity was, as we have said, originally felt in judicial decisions dealing with concrete situations, each of them unique, and out of these decisions there gradually developed the general principles embodied in law. To take a very simple illustration from the earliest code, the book of the Covenant:

If a man deliver unto his neighbor an ass or an ox or a sheep or any beast, to keep and it die or be hurt or be driven away no man seeing it, then shall the man swear before Yahweh that he hath not laid hands upon the other man's property; the owner must accept this oath and no restitution shall be made. (Ex. 22:10 f.)

We are already at the stage of codification. Behind the law as it stands, there lie the many different cases in which this kind of situation has been presented as is indicated by the reference to the various possibilities of damage. But even in the form of the law there persists the awareness that God himself is there exercising the power of his righteousness towards a right settlement of the dispute, and human righteousness consists in conformity with the will of God. This sense of the divine activity declaring itself within the law persisted throughout Israel's history. So in the much later body of law known as the Holiness Code we find appended to many of the injunctions the simple statement, "I am the Lord." Notably this is the case with the significant command: "Thou shalt love thy neighbor as thyself." This is much more than the reminder that life stands constantly under the divine scrutiny. It is the assertion that in seeking to obey the commandment to love one's neighbor, one is aligning one's self with that persistent energizing of the will of God that is ever seeking to draw human beings into closer and more understanding fellowship. So it is that even when we have found an answer to the often difficult problem of what love of our neighbor demands, if we are aware of the presence of God in the situation, we cannot but feel that our best behavior falls short of entering into that love of his in which he is calling us to participate. No doubt, some of you will be thinking in this connection of our Lord's words, "When you shall have done all those things which are commanded you, say, We are unprofitable servants: we have done that which was our duty to do."

Doubtless still later than the putting together of the Holiness Code was the composition of the 119th Psalm. That psalm with its elaborate acrostic form and its constant repetition of the words "statutes," "commandments," "judgments," "testimonies," seems to many people a highly artificial composition hardly to be thought of as poetry, and rather a dry document as far as religion is concerned. But it is to be noted that after the first three verses it is invariably the second person singular that is used.

The writer is addressing God. "I will thank *thee* with an unfeigned heart when I shall have learned the judgment of *thy* righteousness" (119:7). "I will talk of *thy* commandments and have respect unto *thy* ways" (119:15). The psalm was composed by one who was, so to speak, on his knees in the presence of God. Through the commandments and the statutes and the testimonies God is speaking and, as in the case of every divine utterance, there is more in it than can be put into words. So the psalmist more than once prays that his eyes may be opened to see the wondrous things of thy law (119:18). But even more than that because, as we have noted, the word is the active extension of the divine presence; through his commandments God is felt to draw nearer to man in his own person. The divine activity ever pressing forward through the law is one with that which sustains the universe in being. "Thou hast laid the foundations of the earth and it abideth. They continue this day according to thine ordinance for all things serve thee." (119:90 f.) And again: "The earth O Lord is full of thy mercy. O teach me thy statutes" (119:64). And so the writer can declare: "Thy word hath quickened me" (119:50). The word of God does not simply present a claim—it is life giving. The mood of the psalm as a whole alternates strangely between what seems, until we note the context, undue satisfaction in moral achievement—"I have thought upon thy Name, O Lord, in the night season and have kept thy law" (119:55)—and a sometimes troubled, sometimes joyous, awareness of the depth upon depth of the divine goodness which the writer feels himself called upon to explore. "Thou art my portion, O Lord. I have promised to keep thy law I made my humble petition in thy presence with my whole heart. O be merciful unto thy servant according to thy word" (vv. 57, 58). But on the other hand, "Thy statutes have been my songs in the house of my pilgrimage" (v. 54). "O give me understanding that I may learn thy commandments." Always there is the sense of vision and power that the awareness of the divine righteousness at work within the world can give, and always, too, the realization of the something infinitely more, the participation to which God's righteousness is constantly summoning us. Always it is to be kept in mind that it is the transcendent God who is immanent within the longing and the struggle for goodness, and in the moral precepts that cover our fumbling ignorance, self-centered and ready to see just that in any situation which will serve its own interest; but the transcendent God is never included within the process or within the law. Something like this, doubtless, was what Martin Luther had in mind when he wrote: "He who merely studies the commandment of God is not greatly moved, but he who listens to God commanding—how can he fail to be terrified by majesty so great?"

To listen to God commanding is, in the first place, humbly to acknowledge that in any given situation God is present not as it were simply in the background, waiting to overrule the evil that men do to the eventual fulfillment of his righteousness, but actively at work in the course of events. Here we are human beings, exercising the freedom with which he has endowed us and using or abusing the energies and the abilities that he is likewise bestowing upon us. Of all these actual and potential experiences and interests, he is taking account; and within and through the play of conflicting forces he is both declaring his will and taking into its consummation all that is genuinely honest and good in human effort and desire.

But the God commanding, to whom we thus listen, is always the transcendent God. The factors to be reckoned with are not simply those already given, as if the end result could be reached only in a kind of readjustment of forces by a process of give and take. That would be to think of God as included within the situation and to forget the inexhaustible creative energy of him who is continually making all things new, as all that is, moment by moment, is carried forward into the future.

The difficulty of keeping clearly in mind both the divine immanence and the divine transcendence comes most clearly to light when, as in the Advent season, the effort is made to picture the end, the final fulfillment that is inevitably to come. There are those who insist that the ultimate manifestation of God's majesty and righteousness and love lies utterly beyond history. They seem thus to make almost nugatory the human struggle to order the course of the world in accordance with the demands of justice and love, and to rob the process of history of much of its meaning.

On the other hand, there are those who, much less hopefully than a generation ago, picture a gradual improvement of this world order which shall ultimately reach a goal on which the seal of the divine approval can finally be set. In both approaches there is little vision of the marvelous transfiguration of this dear familiar earth, so freighted with human joy and sorrow, that the transcendent power of the always immanent God can bring to pass.

Perhaps we may dare to ask what it may mean to be sensitive to what God is saying and doing in this time of stress and disillusionment. We are often told that God has come in judgment upon a world in which human selfishness and greed and arrogance and pride have taken possession of his gifts, and used them for their own ends, in utter disregard of the claims of his righteousness and love. And those of us whose memories go back to the early days of this century can recall the degree to which material prosperity had been made the be-all and end-all of existence and the smug complacency of many of those who were able to achieve this prosperity, are bound to admit that in many ways the world was ripe for judgment.

But the mode of God's judgment is the all-important question. It is not as if sitting aloof from the scene, he is simply condemning the failure to order life in accordance with standards of righteousness which he has established and is then sending punishment upon a hopelessly guilty world. His own righteousness, the energy of his will, is ceaselessly making for the good, for that which—taking account of the whole situation, of the strange mingling of good and evil in human decision and effort—will make for the ultimate fulfillment of his loving purpose for his world. This does indeed involve destruction, for there is so much in the way of pride in achievement and unreality in professed ideals that stands between man and his Maker that there come times when only a radical purging of life can provide free course for the divine creativity and so our God can reveal himself, in the words of the Epistle to the Hebrews, as a consuming fire.

But it is not, as such words seem to say, that over against human achievement God's righteousness is at work, as if he must reduce man to abject and pitiable helplessness before he can find his way into human life. The author of those wonderful letters from prison, Dietrich Bonhoeffer, reminds us again and again that God is the "beyond" in the midst of life, not where human powers give out on the border, but in the center of human accomplishment and joy in living. To listen to God commanding in the present crisis is to look for signs of his declaring his activity in what is actually being brought to pass by human effort, and in aspirations and purposes that are pressing for realization. We should all agree, of course, that what God is doing and saying is not to be identified either with the Voice of America or the *Pravda* editorials. We are not of those who look for peaceable coexistence if it can be arrived at as a state of wishful waiting for the other side's total collapse. In some measures ours is something of the attitude of Abraham Lincoln in the distressful days of the Civil War. At the time when the Emancipation Proclamation was in the writing, John Hay found on the President's desk a meditation written only for his own eye. Had not the young secretary made a copy of it, we should never have known the hidden struggles of that mind at that hour. Here are the words:

The will of God prevails. In great contests each party claims to act in accordance with the will of God. Both may be, and one must be, wrong. God cannot be for and against the same thing at the same time. In the present civil war it is quite possible that God's purpose is something different from the purposes of either party, and yet the human instrumentalities working just as they do are the best adaptation to effect this purpose.

One is reminded of that great saying of Joab, the ruthless warrior and hard-headed statesman of David's time. Faced with the enemy on two points, he bade his troops: "Be of good courage and let us play the men for our people and for the cities of our God, and the Lord do that which seemeth him good." That goes to the very heart of the Old Testament in its teaching about God, acknowledging his transcendence and recognizing also the worth of human effort as that through which God will bring about the fulfillment of his purpose.

Of the way in which today through human effort and aspiration the righteousness of God is moving on to the reordering of his world, there is, of course, clear indication in the world-wide awakening of the underprivileged everywhere to a new hope of freedom from destitution, from living, as it were, on the very edge of existence, to a new hope of entering into fulness of life as individuals and as peoples. Let me emphasize that word "peoples," for with all the dangers that inhere in nationalism as pride and selfishness seek to use it for their own ends, there is within it the seeking for the realization of what belonging may mean in the enjoyment of those distinctive values of one's own group life, in grateful appreciation of which one finds the enhancement of one's own being and deliverance from the loneliness of one's soul. To recognize this is to understand that the surging tide of new energy, of human aspiration for a good life, is not merely a matter of bread-and-butter existence but a craving for a more abundant life as human beings, in the full sense of the word. Even the monstrous evil of which power-hungry leaders are capable, as they play upon the fears and hopes of humble lives, cannot blind us to the awakening of new life behind the Iron Curtain, where millions have been lifted out of illiteracy into richer participation in life's values. Admit again the dangers and abuses which these same power-hungry leaders are making of it, and still there is the need for acknowledging God's righteousness at work in bringing to vast numbers of ignorant peasants at least a partial appreciation of what it may mean to participate in the great cultural heritage of that which Dostoevski was fond of calling, "Holy Russia."

In thus discerning the activity of the divine righteousness declaring itself in the lifting of life to a new level, which does not mean only what we call raising the standard of living, we are true to that Old Testament understanding of the divine righteousness, which thinks of it so frequently as concern for the underprivileged and the dispossessed. I need not remind you of the prophet's unsparing denunciation of the brutal oppression of the poor as offering primary evidence of rebellion against God. Just to take two passages from the book of Isaiah. On the lips of the prophet, God himself hurls this challenge in the face of the rich and powerful of that day:

> Ye have devoured the vineyard,
> The spoil of the poor is in your houses,
> What mean ye that ye beat my people to pieces
> And grind the faces of the poor. (3:14, 15)

And, at a much later time when Israel's life as a nation had come to an end, an unknown prophet finds the hope for the future for a despairing fragment of a people in the divine announcement:

> I bring near my righteousness,
> It shall be not far off
> And my salvation shall not tarry. (46:13)

Here again the association of God's righteousness and salvation is to be noted, emphasizing as it does the dynamic character of that righteousness, the energizing movement of God's will in the flowing into life of that which makes for the rich unfolding of life's meaning and possibilities. So in the same book God again speaks by the mouth of another unknown prophet:

> There is no God beside me,
> A just God [a righteous God]
> and a Savior. (45:21)

And the difficulty commentators generally feel about thinking of God in the same breath as both righteous and savior is re-solved if it is remembered that to think of God as righteous is to think of him as engaged in positive constructive activity that must ultimately issue in success and victory, and so the passage continues: "Look unto me and be ye saved, share in my victory, all the ends of the earth."

So, too, whenever men of good will feel upon their pulses the pitiful craving of fellow human beings for more abundant life, and in glad surrender, no matter what the cost, strive to give of themselves and their abilities as those who in very truth draw upon the inexhaustible riches of God's goodness, there is a participation in the all-conquering movement of God's own righteousness in his world.

Only here, too, there is danger that it be forgotten that it is this movement of the will of the transcendent God in which one is allowed to participate. For example, there can be no question that in the great words "truth," "justice," "freedom," there are unmistakable indications of God's way among men. The danger lies in the temptation to identify our own under-standing of these terms with God's meaning and thus to give our interpretation of them an absolute value. All men of good will are, indeed, called to bring to the consideration of the ap-plication of the principles of truth, justice, and freedom to the problems of human living all the wisdom that they possess, but they must remember, too, that just because these terms are not abstractions but modes of activity of the transcendent God of all power and might, he is never to be enclosed within any human reading of them. To treat these great words, as if in complete possession of all that they can mean, so that, for example, the American way of life is held to represent them so completely as to constitute a world standard—this is to forget the infinite overtones in what God is saying and doing and to take advantage of his immanent activity to make him, so to speak, entirely our own.

In so many ways even the best intentioned people can yield to the temptation to put in a claim to make the very condescension of God instrumental for the realization of their own ideas and interests. Do not we ourselves know that this is often true of the manner of our approach to God in our prayers, that almost unawarely we are engaged in trying to bend the divine will in accordance with our own outlook and desire? I know of no more pathetic instance of what this means than is to be found in Georges Bernanos' moving *Diary of a Country Priest*. In a desperate crisis the young priest finds himself praying, as he puts it, "with a kind of savage, concentrated violence in a sheer transport of will." And he goes on to say: "I wanted to have God to myself. He did not come to me."

Before we go on to consider the relationship of the transcendence of God to his immanent activity as it found expression in the ministry of the prophets, we must take account of yet another factor in Israel's understanding of God's revelation of himself. Life in Canaan meant a change from the pastoral life of the nomad to the settled life of tillers of the soil, and this introduced into Israel's religion a new sense of Yahweh's power as manifested in the life of nature. In Canaan the prevailing religion was a form of nature worship. In each little district the local *numen*, the Baal supreme within a circumscribed area, absorbed the devotion of its inhabitants. He brought to a focus all the life-giving force of that particular region. The fertility of man and beast and tree and plant derived from him. It was he that gave his worshipers corn and wine and oil. It was preeminently a religion of the soil. With this religion of the land Israel's religion had to come to terms. With the fertility rites at the shrines, involving gross sensuality, and with the magic and witchcraft that also sought to subject the divine to human manipulation, Israel's spiritual leaders could make no compromise. These practices were the expression of something that lay at the heart of Baalism, the localization of deity, giving assurance that the divine was, so to speak, stabilized and could, therefore, be possessed, an object of calculation and control. At the same time, in spite of the fundamental antagonism between Yahwism and Baalism, there was that in the religion of the land which could deepen and enrich the sense of God's relationship to the life of man. In the recognition of the divine at work within the day-by-day processes of the world of nature there was given a realization of God's ordered ways and of his tender concern for man as shown in nature's ministration to human welfare. In such a saying as, "While the earth remaineth, seedtime and harvest, and cold and heat, and summer and winter, and day and night shall not cease" (Gen. 8.22), the ordered round of the seasons is felt to be immediately dependent on the divine will. At the risk of oversimplification it may be said that to early Israel had been given a profound sense of the creative movement of God's will in history, while in Canaan men had come to a deep awareness of the persistent and pervasive movement of the divine energy in nature; and one element in the greatness of Israel's religion is to be found in its insistence on the interfusion of these two sides of God's immanent activity.

In contrast with this we may think of the failure of Christian leaders and teachers in the ninetenth century to take account of the light thrown by scientific inquiry on the mode of God's immanent activity. Indeed, we still need, for example, that more generous attitude toward evolutionary theory in the realm of nature or history which can bring to our religion a deeper awareness of the continuousness and pervasiveness of the divine creativity, while it would make clearer some of the limitations of that theory. For the only kind of criticism of the results of honest inquiry that is worth while is that which has first sought to understand that inquiry from within and assess its positive value. For criticism and modification of any theory that thinks to have said the ultimate word and that, as it were, takes life completely under human control (as sometimes seems to be the position of a certain type of humanism) is as necessary today as it was in the course of Israel's history. For with that people the recognition of God at work in nature did bring with it the tendency to *identify* him with the processes of that same nature. In the religion of the land this tendency had resulted in the conviction that the *numen* of any particular district, embodying all the forces, spiritual and material, of that locality, was so far included within these forces as to be incapable of exercising power else- where. So many in Israel came to think of Yahweh as the god of the land. The whole of Israel's territory was, to be sure, his domain. But other lands were outside the sphere of his interest, if not of his power. So folk tradition made even David speak of Saul's attempt to drive him from the inherit- ance of Yahweh as equivalent to a command to "go serve other gods" (1 Sam. 26:19). Together with this reducing of Yahweh to the level of a Baal, involving the belief that the activity of deity immanent in the order of nature was simply to serve human ends and could be made entirely subject to human control, Israel's deeply rooted sense of a privileged re- lationship to God had become the further ground for thinking of God as identified with their own interests. It was he who had brought them into the good land of Canaan and made them a nation. He had, so they thought, chosen them for their own advantage. They could think of him as bound up with their destiny; his unique greatness could be regarded as a national asset. So Yahweh's activity in the order of history had come to be considered as simply making for the advance- ment of Israel's interests no matter what might be the character of the national life. The prophet Micah must denounce the ravenous greed of the leaders of the people:

> Judges passing verdicts for a bribe,
> Priests giving oracles for pay,
> Prophets divining for money
> All the while saying, Is not the Lord among us,
> None evil can come upon us. (2:11)

Amos taunts those who lightheartedly hail the day of Yahweh's final manifestation of power as the day of the fulfillment of their own fondest hopes:

> Woe unto you that desire the day of Yahweh,
> What shall the day of Yahweh mean to you?
> It is darkness and not light,
> Even thick darkness with no gleam of light therein.
> (5-18, 20)

The same prophet contrasts the jaunty tone of the round of festival and sacrifice, with its pleasure-loving readiness to make God participant in its enjoyment as if he were one of them, with the series of dread visitations of famine, drought, pestilence, and earthquake with which the God they thus so cheerfully worshipped had summoned his people to repentance. Or again, Isaiah holds up to scorn those who can blasphemously dare God to be anything but a friendly divinity. Pray let us see what he will do, let him make haste. We'd like to know what the Holy One of Israel has in mind.

So when the great prophets of the eighth and seventh centuries announce that God is about to destroy his people for their sins, they are essentially proclaiming the freedom of God from the entangling hold upon him that men had sought to establish. These prophets looked into the face of tragedy, saw life at its darkest, and were sustained in their harsh ministry by their certainty that the transcendent power, the majesty, the righteousness of God would be vindicated as the ultimate triumphant reality, that righteousness must prevail even at the cost of the ruin of their world. Here was that which surpassed all merely human hopes and aspirations, seeming even to deny their value and the possibility of their realization. Of what lay beyond destruction in the terms of human living, it was not theirs to know. Enough for the great prophets of doom that the righteous will of God would have its way. Zeal for the honor of God consumed them.

To be sure, the transcendent sovereignty of God that they proclaimed did not stand out of all relationship to human activity. The great Assyrian and Babylonian empires were the instruments of his will, though in the end their pride and arrogance would subject them to judgment and they, too, would perish. But even more than this, for the prophets themselves there was the consciousness that power from on high had laid hold of their own lives, and in and through their surrender to the infinitely greater than themselves, God was still at work in his world. But for them the catastrophic aspect of his activity was the dominant one. "Is not my word like fire, like a hammer that breaketh the rocks in pieces?" is the way in which, upon the lips of Jeremiah, God characterized the effect of his ingress into life through the ministry of the prophet. The manifestation of transcendent power is so overwhelming as to obliterate consideration of the actuality of God's immanent activity in the years gone by or what he may do in his world in the days to come. In the blazing light of the fire of the divine righteousness the whole history of the past seemed so infected with arrogant pride and grasping greed as to make it appear nothing but the record of pitiful human failure.

Yet a notable feature of the Old Testament, taken as a whole, is its unfaltering insistence on the worth of the present order and an eager looking forward to what the future holds in store for human life. The earth shall be full of the knowledge of the Lord as the waters cover the sea. And the work of righteousness shall be peace and the effect of righteousness, quietness and assurance for ever. As one of the ablest of Old Testament scholars, H. Wheeler Robinson, has put it: "Within the present world order and on the stage of human history God will be finally victorious." His will is to be done on earth. Alongside of the oracles that announce impending doom there are many others that speak of a glorious future for Israel and for the part it is to play in the accomplishment of God's great purpose for his world. Reconciliation of the two very different outlooks upon life, that of the great prophets whose names we know and that of the anonymous prophecies of a glorious future, is in some measure achieved by the recognition on the part of Biblical criticism that the oracles of hope belong to a time subsequent to the fulfillment of the prophecies of doom, that is to say, to a time after the fall of Jerusalem in 586 B.C. Some of these oracles of hope, however, belong to an earlier time and nearly all of them, no doubt, had independent currency before they came to their present position in the books of the prophets. What is only now being realized is that their origin is quite other than that of the prophecies that announce catastrophic disaster; that whereas there were the utterances of great individuals remarkable for the way in which they stood over against the life of their day, keenly aware of the immediacy of their relationship to the God of all righteousness, a relationship which set them apart from their fellows in tragic loneliness, the oracles of hope came from those who were members of a group and in that fellowship found themselves in close and intimate touch with the national life, the hopes, and aspirations of a people. In the light of the great prophets' proclamation of the transcendent righteousness of God, these group prophets lift a people's hopes and aspiration to a new level of spiritual vision. The story of the four hundred prophets in I Kings 22 affords impressive illustration of the connection and the contrast between the two types of prophecy. With one accord the four hundred declare that Yahweh will deliver Ramoth-gilead into the hands of Ahab. One of their number in particular, Zedekiah ben Chenaanah, by his behavior and utterance, gives dramatic expression to the group consciousness. With horns of iron he represents the passes for religion is but the most formal and conventional recognition of God. Even where people seem to be groping for better things, it is so often a kind of spiritual egoism, a simple desire for self-realization that knows pitifully little about God and sometimes seems to care even less. And so there is laid upon us the necessity of proclaiming the reality of the supernatural or the transcendent in such a way as to keep clearly before men the awful holiness of God's righteousness and love. That is our primary task, but it can be done only as, at the same time, we keep ourselves deeply sensitive to the strain and stress of life's struggle, as we enter into the longings and aspirations of human hearts, whether it be those of the group of our own people or, as the circle widens, those of the community at large or of the national life or, again, of a world in distress and conflict. So we can discern, even in self-assertion and pride, in people's inordinate insistence on their own interests, the perversion of God-given instinct and desire; and as we place ourselves at the heart of human striving, we must seek to open to others the vision of what life may be if effort and aspirations are brought into the right relation to the energizing will of the righteous, loving God. For we are priests of One in whom, as I shall presently point out, both types of prophecy find their glorious reconciliation; and it is ours as God gives us power to maintain a due proportion and balance between them. Each of us must do it in his own way, and I am hoping that, as I turn back to the prophets, I may say something that will be of help in doing this.

The outstanding example of the group type of prophecy is, of course, to be found in the fortieth and following chapters of the Book of Isaiah. It is significant that the opening oracle, "Comfort ye, comfort ye my people," is addressed to others who can exercise a like ministry with the speaker. He is thus marked as one of a company. Not his the lonely ministry of a Jeremiah. Indeed, in view of the frequent changes in tone in the utterances that follow and the obvious lack of direct con-

nection in many cases, it may be asked whether this section of
the book of Isaiah does not represent the bringing together of
the sayings of not one or two unknown prophets, but of many
who stood in the great Isaiah tradition. However that may be,
the note that prevails throughout is one of a profound sense of
the intimacy of Israel's relationship to Yahweh, with a consequent, compelling insistence on the reality of God's immanent
activity in the history of Israel from the time of the call of
Abraham; but all this as part of the way in which God will ful-
fill his purpose of bringing all men to the knowledge of himself.
God's choice of Israel is, therefore, set against the background
of the manifestation of his power as Creator and Sustainer of
the universe and in the context of a world history that is under
his guidance and control.

> Thus saith the Lord that created the heavens; God himself
> that formed the earth and made it; he established it; he created
> it not in vain, he formed it to be inhabited: I am the Lord and
> there is none else. . . . I said not unto the house of Jacob, Seek ye me
> in vain: I the Lord speak righteousness, I declare things that are
> right. (45:18, 19)
> I have sworn by myself, the word is gone out of my mouth in
> righteousness, and shall not return, That unto me every knee shall
> bow, every tongue shall swear. (45:23)

This lifting of human aspiration to new heights of vision
and new depth of understanding comes to its climax in the
series of poems, known as the Servant Poems. The first of
these poems introduces, as you will remember, in dramatic
form One whom God names his servant.

> Behold my servant, whom I uphold;
> My chosen one, in whom my soul delighteth,
> I have endowed him with my spirit:
> To carry true religion to the Gentiles. (42:1)

There follows then the Servant's wondering, almost awestruck
recognition of the greatness of the mission thus entrusted to
him. He had known himself endowed with especial gifts and

light of the divine transcendence, lifts to a new level the longing of the faithful remnant for the fulfillment of their life's
meaning in the exercise of the great spiritual gifts committed
to them. But one thing yet remained to be dealt with. The
very consciousness of spiritual endowment could so easily become an intense self-consciousness. They could think of
God's final victory only in the terms of their own leadership,
in an Israel brought back to full and loyal acceptance of the
great truth for which they stood, the hope of the future being
bound up with their own existence. It was only in the humble
acceptance of the fact of death that the last vestige of self that
centered on the importance of their own preservation could be
purged away and God's own righteousness have free course
into his world at large. The transcendent God makes known
the riches of his inexhaustible saving power, not only in the
mysterious depths of life but in the mystery of death accepted
as the final and complete committing of self into his hands.

Father, into thy hands I commend my spirit.

That last word from the Cross strikes home to our hearts,
reminds us that it is in none other than the Christ that the two
lines of prophecy find their complete reconciliation and fulfillment. The divine transcendence that again and again in the
convulsions of nature, in the ministry of the great prophets
had broken in upon human life, shattering human hopes and
expectations as these sought to subordinate God to self-
centered plans and purposes, that divine transcendence made
its supreme breaking in upon this life of ours when the Word
became flesh and dwelt among us. But the human life into
which the Son of God thus entered was instinct with the presence and power of God's continuous immanent activity. We
think of the group pictured in the first two chapters of
St. Luke, Zacharias and Elizabeth, Simeon and Anna, and,
above all, Mary the expectant mother. We enter into the spirit
of the *Magnificat* and the *Nunc Dimittis,* and we realize how
wonderful had been the preparation for our Lord's coming so

that his human nature could be the fulfillment of all that the persistent pervasive activity of God's righteousness had been striving to make of human life. In Jesus Christ every moment presents its dread, baffling challenge of the divine perfectness of beauty, truth, and goodness, as he summons us to take up the cross, forsake all and follow him, while yet he is continuously with us, our companion and our friend, our unfailing stay and support, he in us and in our people, the immanent Christ; we and they in him, our transcendent Lord; he humbled himself and became obedient unto death, even the death of the Cross.

Wherefore God also hath highly exalted him, and given him a name that is above every name: That at the name of Jesus every knee should bow, of things in heaven, and things in earth, and things under the earth; and that every tongue should confess that Jesus Christ is Lord, to the glory of God the Father. (Phil. 2:9-10)

❧ The One Foundation:

The Dean's Installation Sermon

For other foundation can no man lay than that is laid, which is Jesus Christ.— 1 Cor. 3:11

These are the words that come often and instinctively to our lips as we of today take our part in the great and noble heritage that has come down to us. That is surely what they would have us say into whose labors we have entered. Into the fashioning of this Institution's hundred years of loyal service have gone the unremitting toil of faithful servants of God, the generous giving of large-hearted benefactors, the wise planning of devoted minds, the reverent thought of able scholars, the high aspirations of generation after generation of young hearts aglow with the enthusiasm of entrance upon holy service, the prayers of countless devout souls; and all these have been woven into a living unity in Christ. And in him they live who have given and planned and taught and learned and prayed, and of their life in him we partake. It is not simply that we reap the advantage of their toil, the residuum of their earthly existence now that they are removed from the scene. It is the glory of the Christian faith that for the Church of the living God there is no dead past. All glows and palpitates with life pressing eagerly and insistently upon

50

the future, touching with the radiance of eternity the fleeting moment that we call the present and giving even to our brief years of troubled aspiration a worth that has no end. "To whom coming, as unto a living stone, disallowed indeed of men, but chosen of God, and precious," we "also, as lively stones, are built up a spiritual house, a holy priesthood, to offer up spiritual sacrifices acceptable to God by Jesus Christ."

This is not said merely because a reverent and grateful acknowledgment of the labors of others is the fitting mood at such a time as this. Herein lies the first and necessary premise for any consideration of the problem of theological education. Amid all the confused questionings and bewildering doubts and perplexities which beset our day this at least stands fast for those who believe in theology at all. God has revealed himself to human hearts and minds. It is his holy reality with which we begin, a reality given in the world of nature all about us, in history, in the discipline of a chosen people, in the life and death and rising again of Jesus Christ, in the work of the Holy Spirit uniting men in the fellowship of the Church; and all this is set forth for us concretely in the living tradition of this Seminary in which God has given us a part. We build upon a certainty. Our city hath foundations. We begin not with theory but with fact. "God has claimed us all in Christ as his sons." It is this givenness of basic fact in the acknowledgment of which we are faced with God's self-revealing that distinguishes theology from that religion which is today appropriately called comparative. In quite impartial ways the students of this latter-day science explore the darker recesses of psychology, gather their data from the remote and obscure regions of anthropology, hail with delight every survival of the primitive and barbarous. We are profoundly indebted to them, for the results of their investigations serve to throw new light on the hidden treasures of the Christian faith and reveal in unexpected ways the universality of the human need which that faith alone can meet. But in so far as they themselves dis-

regard the great outstanding facts of revelation and pride
themselves on their detachment from tradition they arrive
only at a mysterious something, a nameless god, unknown
and unknowable. But we have a sure word of witness that enables us to "speak that we do know and testify that we have
seen."

Our primary concern then is with a great tradition. It is to
the deeper understanding and explication of this that our
energies are first of all directed. We do not in the first place
create or imagine or devise, we seek to interpret that which is
given. We do not even begin by seeking evidence for its truth.
We desire to understand it as it is. God has spoken, is speaking, and we listen eagerly that we may miss no syllable of his
utterance. "Speak, Lord, for thy servant heareth" is the cry
in our hearts. For it is an enterprise to challenge all our powers, this elucidation of a splendid tradition of life. It is easy
enough to be a traditionalist and catch up phrases of the past
and make their frequent repetition the badge of orthodoxy;
but to grow into the larger life that has created these phrases,
to learn to look out upon the world in all its manifold variety,
its seemingly chaotic struggle, in the light thrown upon it by
God's revelation of himself, to feel the thrill as well as hold the
theory of the universe as God's universe and the Church as
the body of our Lord, this would be impossible if it were a task
for the brain alone. Study will do much, is of course indispensable, the kind of intensive concentrated study that theological students are singularly loath to give, but it must be
study supported and sustained by prayer, enriched and made
creative by worship. For the end that we seek is freedom, freedom of the domain of the spirit, the franchise of the Kingdom,
the liberty of the Catholic faith, the power to deal consistently
with life in the terms of the great Christian truths, not simply
by direct and conscious focusing of the mind so that in face of
a crisis we are not worried and nervous about the correct-
ness of our procedure but with an instinctive loyalty that can,

as occasion demands, meet the emergency with that originality which shall reveal anew the astounding richness of the old truths. We tend in these days to alternate between two slaveries, the slavery of the letter and the slavery of our own moods. We seem shut up to a choice between a cold precision, void of life, and an intense sensationalism that has no meaning or value beyond itself, a mere surface play of emotion. Are not both the result of the shallowness of our thought, our failure to enter into the fulness of our heritage, to draw upon all the resources of our faith? We may learn here surely from one who went not with us. "Deep minds," says Goethe, "are compelled to live in the past as well as in the future."

If, then, I plead for a more intensive attack upon the ancient disciplines of theology, for a devotional knowledge of the Bible which shall have entered through the gate of criticism into its life and spirit, for such an understanding of dogmatic theology and history as shall lead men anew to go behind phrases and events and feel the way in which, in and through them all, the living God has been teaching and disciplining his children, let it not be supposed that I am oblivious of the urgent demands made upon the priesthood of today for service in many fields. The priest of the Church is to work in this modern world, and to win men for Christ he must be sensitive to the perplexities and the needs of this present age. Let us face the problem fairly in all its complexity. Here are social, economic, political questions upon which he must have a mind of his own, which yet must be in some way the mind of Christ. Or in another direction there is the appeal of the individual soul as expressed in the quest for healing of mind and body. Whether that is to take the form of psychotherapy or that weird psychoanalysis which Freud has brought to our attention, simple ignorance may mean forfeiting that opportunity to serve which the priest of God must always crave. Or again, child study clamors for attention. There is a new ferment in the world of education. Can the priest hold aloof and refuse to heed the cry of the little ones? Some few there will be who feel themselves called to select one of these needs of our modern life as an especial field of endeavor, and it is altogether right that as ministers of Jesus Christ they should take their place among these self-sacrificing laborers for the sake of what they can give and the first-hand knowledge which they can thus gain for the Church. But if such men are to be more than, for example, social service experts, if they are actually to give to those with whom they work new understanding and broader vision, if they are to enable these devoted workers to derive their inspiration more directly from our Lord, if they are to be saved themselves from that narrowing of interest which waits upon the footsteps of the specialist in any department; if, in other words, they are to make the distinctive contribution that their priesthood should enable them to give, they must above all be possessed of that intensive living knowledge of the depth and meaning of the Christian faith of which I have been speaking, even though the time spent in winning it prolongs the period of their preparation. In these days there are many who think of religion as social morality touched with emotion and lose in well-meaning sympathy the power to see the greatness of men's souls and the look of eternity in their eyes. It is when the priest comes to them as an ambassador of Christ knowing what his Lord doeth that he makes his true contribution to their need and work.

Then for the great majority of the clergy who cannot and ought not to be experts in any one of these fields and yet should have some knowledge of them all and for this must be dependent in large measure on the results of others' investigations, what shall save them from falling prey to the latest theory, subservient followers of those with whom the last cry has become a shrill yell? There is in the loyal and faithful understanding of the Church's life, in the pervasion of soul and mind with the working of the Holy Spirit, such a contact with reality as gives discernment, the ability to distinguish between true and false even when they are so closely intermingled as in so many of the movements of our own day. It is not mere acquaintance with new theories with power to add to their number that we need. Sympathetic insight is the necessary thing. With this, we shall neither hold coldly aloof nor commit ourselves headlong to the latest program; but, quietly and simply, more by patient representation than by vehement assertion, we shall enable men to perceive the difference that Christ makes. The approach should doubtless be indicated in seminary days, lectures perhaps given, the right books pointed out, but in the brief time at our disposal it is principles upon which the emphasis must be laid and principles so wedded with life that they may be applied flexibly in many directions.

It is, in a word, character, the character of members of the Body of Christ that is all-important; and character as we know in this time of insistence upon the unity of personality is a matter of thinking as well as of doing, of the instincts and the affections as well as of the will. It is the power to function freely and naturally in the common life of thought and action because that common life is given from above. What men are feeling after in secular education is but the feeble echo of that which the Church can surely give. "What is needed," says Professor Dewey in his recent book *Democracy and Education,* "is intelligent sympathy or good will. For sympathy as a desirable quality is something more than mere feeling, it is a cultivated imagination for what men have in common and a rebellion at whatever unnecessarily divides them"; and one notes the resemblance, while one feels the difference, in this utterance of a Belgian monk: "The unfailing criterion by which to judge of the value of a thing from the supernatural point of view consists chiefly in this, to examine if it helps or hinders the union of men with God and through God with one another." Here in this Seminary we make the discovery, the reasoned discovery that is to control heart and mind and will, of how rich and fruitful the life of fellowship in Christ may be.

And if this seems to center too much attention upon life as it is to be lived here with too little direct regard to the years of service that lie beyond, it may, I think, fairly be urged that so long as the great purpose is kept in view men will best prepare for it by devoted application to the full opportunity of the present. So much of what may be said of the future bears the aspect of theory, lies in the realm of hypothesis, while the present has a living actuality. When all is said the theological seminary cannot quite be classified with the professional schools. It is life itself with which the priest is to deal, and in living we shall find the way. At Harvard they have been trying to discover whether the study of economics is of greater value for good citizenship or for vocational efficiency. Even there it is only for the purposes of analysis that the distinction can be maintained. There can be no really good citizenship that does not include vocational efficiency, no true vocational efficiency that is not a part of good citizenship. For us certainly the one passes almost inevitably into the other. Good citizenship in the Kingdom of God, if the word "good" be not emptied of its meaning, should enable a man to give account of his stewardship. For true goodness recognizes responsibilities and is a quality of the mind as well as of the heart. "What men call simple goodness," said Bishop Paget, "is under very complex conditions of work not so simple or obvious a matter as it sounds. The unembarrassed insight that goes straight to the real character of an action or suggestion, the just imagination which can enter into another's position, the kindly shrewdness which is never credulous and never cynical, the strength of mind that can resist the temptation to be clever, and, above all, that sense of things unseen which makes palpable the folly of ever fancying that there can be through evil a short cut to good."

Simple goodness, wise with the wisdom that is from above, understanding what the will of the Lord is—that has been sought and found here by the help of the Holy Spirit. Priests whose lips keep knowledge, true messengers of the Lord of Hosts, have gone forth from this Seminary. And in humble reliance upon the selfsame Spirit we go forward.

❧ The Challenge of the Ministry to Young Men

What has the Church to say to the young man of generous ideals, who has discovered that in the service of others is to be found the truest realization of life's opportunities? There are so many agencies which offer him scope for the use of disinterested talents, from the Y.M.C.A. to community welfare work in its varied forms. Law and medicine as well as teaching hold the promise of rich return in the way of contribution to the common weal. Does the Church offer more than any of these when it asks young men to serve in the sacred ministry? The answer has in it the note of challenge.

The Church offers more, far more, because it claims more. It asks for the complete consecration of the whole man because it will set him in effective relation with the whole of human life. In its service everything counts, all that a man has said and is and has the possibility of being, because he is to be made the vehicle of that love of Christ for man which will penetrate with its power all that the world is or may become. The especial gift finds its distinctive opportunity, but not as separate from the rest of a man's being. The ministry claims the whole of a man for the whole of God's world. It is this universality of claim and outlook that is both the challenge and the reward. Other agencies for good must necessarily handle problems in partial and fragmentary ways, dealing with particular aspects of life; for them men and women inevitably fall into classes, sick or well, good or bad citizens, above or below the line of comfortable subsistence, educated or uneducated, radical or reactionary. For the ministry these and many other classifications all have their meaning and are to be reckoned with; but they are seen against the background of all men's surpassing value as children of God, one in their common possession of his great gift of life, one in their common need of a realization of his holiness and power and goodness. Emerson said, perhaps somewhat too scornfully, that no one could long live with reformers and keep his sagacity; and he was doubtless thinking of the way in which in reform movements this or that side of people is thrown into disproportionate relief. The Church alone is concerned with human life in its entirety, all its hopes and fears, its joys and sorrows, its achievements and failures. The priest of the Church, therefore, finds himself set fairly in the center of the marvelous play of human experience in all its fulness. This central position carries with it an insistent demand on his every faculty and brings, too, a rich reward in the way of deep and sane understanding of the meaning of life. It may seem to those who have not realized what is involved in the Incarnation of our Lord that religion is a narrow specialism, touching experience at but one point—so its own votaries have sometimes seemed to think and to hold—but at its best (and the generous-hearted young man will be prepared to take it at its best) the Christian religion seeks to gather within itself the whole of human experience in the whole of the universe. In this process of redeeming not this or that side of life but all of it, the Christ will use men who will yield themselves wholly to him with all their powers of mind and soul and body so that, through human lives thus dedicated, he may become, indeed, the Lord of all good life.

It is perhaps only another way of emphasizing this fundamental truth of the ministry's concern with the whole of life, to point out that religion alone deals with life at its very source. This it is that gives the ministry so central a significance. It has often been urged by the socialist, in speaking of philanthropic reforms, that they are but palliatives, treating symptoms of social disorder but not touching the root causes —"economic" as the socialist describes them—of which these evils are the result. The Church urges that we must go deeper still, that behind the economic causes there is the human factor. It would recognize the truth in H. G. Wells' contention, that all schemes and plans for the reorganization of society must fail in so far as men of good will are wanting. But to touch men's wills, to quicken not their desires simply but their resolution, to give them power, to realize their dreams and aspirations, who is sufficient for these things? They can only be done by bringing men into union with God through Christ that in the fellowship of his Church they may feel the compelling power of his love. Quite recently a popular weekly which prides itself upon its wide dissemination of opinion has been seeking to commend itself to new readers by its claim to meet fundamental needs of human nature. Behind the flamboyant language of its advertisement there is keen insight into what men and women really want. It describes these fundamental needs as just two: the need to discover the way to see into the heart of the world, and the need to make contact with the source of power. Quite simply, these are just the things that the Church has to give. It reveals at the heart of the world the crucified Christ triumphant, the ultimate meaning of life's mystery; and it offers, in union with him, contact with the very source of power, the God of love himself. For the application of this truth and this power to all the thronging problems of our modern world, it needs men, young men, strong men, who, learning themselves to live by this truth, shall in the ministry become the instruments through which the Christ shall gather all men into the joyous fellowship of his great society, the unity of mankind upon which the hopes and dreams of a perplexed and disordered world are set.

⇒ The Education of a Clergyman

Let me begin with the exposition of the title of my talk—
"The Education of a Clergyman." Obviously, it has something to do with theological education. It is inevitable that
what I talk about should be related to that subject, for all my
ministry has been devoted to that field of endeavor. But I am
thinking of something more than seminary training. I have
in mind seminary training as set in the context of the whole
of a man's education, and that of a man called to an especial
kind of leadership in the community. That is why I have
chosen the word "clergyman" rather than either of the great
words "priest" or "minister." These speak specifically of a
man in relation to those whom he immediately serves, and describe therefore, in the first instance, his functional relationship to his own people.

"Clergyman," as it is a more general term, speaks of a man
as he is known by the community at large. It reminds us of
the time when the *clerk*, the man in Orders, was pre-eminently
the man able to read and write, the man of book learning,
and therefore *the* educated man. Something of that association
still clings to the word *clerc* in France, where the term can
be used to describe the savant, the man of letters, as it does
in the title of Julien Benda's notable book *La Trahison des
Clercs*, "The Treachery of the Clerics," in which as early as
1927 he found one great reason for the decline and fall of
Europe in the between-the-war period, the kind of disintegra-

tion recently pictured for us in Bruce Marshall's *Yellow Tapers for Paris*, in the abdication from moral leadership not only of ecclesiastics but of philosophers, teachers, novelists, poets, and writers of every sort. The word "clerk" as he uses it, the word from which "clergyman" is derived, stands for learning and for the responsibility that attaches to the possession of learning. But though many people are still kind enough to regard the clergyman as an educated man, he is, as we well know, no longer thought of as *the* educated man, the learned person of the community. Any number of the people in the pews know far more than he does about a great many subjects. That is a truth which the clergyman will do well to keep constantly in mind, for it will save him from many a rash statement. But the lack of knowledge in some fields, so long as a man knows when he does not know, does not in itself decide whether a man is more or less educated. In fact the question has for some time been asked on every hand whether it is a vast amount of varied information on all sorts and kinds of subjects that constitutes an education. And it has long been felt that a college degree should represent something more than the ability to take one's place as a kind of grown-up quiz kid. As Professor Whitehead has said, "A student should not be taught more than he can think about." So, many years ago it was recognized that there was need of selection, and consequently we have passed through an era when it was held that the wise thing was to let a man choose just the subjects along which his interest lies and give him such knowledge of these as may best fit him for making a living. Thus we have had the era of the elective system, of specialization, and of vocational training. Of course, it must be acknowledged that specialization and vocational training do have their own distinctive values. One who teaches in a theological seminary can hardly afford to think otherwise. But it is increasingly recognized that these do not in themselves produce the educated man. One need not accept the gibe that the specialist is a man who knows more and more about less and less to recognize the danger of serious limitation of outlook to which specialism may lead, a limitation which not infrequently betrays itself in the inability to express oneself in any but one's own jargon. Even theological students are not unknown who have extraordinary facility in their use of conventional religious phraseology and are sadly unable to translate it into a language "understanded of the people." So, even in the realm of theology where, as it deals with ultimate reality, the range of a man's vision should be continuously enlarged, there *may* be a sad narrowing of a man's interests and sympathies and field of understanding. As the Harvard report "General Education in a Free Society" puts it trenchantly, "Specializing in a vocation makes for inflexibility in a world of fluid possibilities."

Recently an Englsh writer, speaking of both American and British universities, has remarked,

The universities profess to be communities of teachers and students united in a search for knowledge and truth; in actual fact there is scarcely a university in which those engaged in the different schools are in fruitful relation with each other: the old unity of knowledge, the belief that such a thing as a Truth about the whole system of things exists and can be found by human minds, has gone. The universities no longer help students to seek for ultimate certainties or for guiding principles.

Over against the fragmentation of life to which our modern education leads so that any sense of direction, of the meaning of the whole, is lost, there is the effort now being made in our colleges to find a way to the recovery of first principles, to the establishment in the mind of the students of the great fundamental truths about life that make for its integration, for belief in the values of living. Of the methods proposed, as institutions set about a complete revision of the curriculum, I cannot venture here to speak. They are many, ranging all the way from Chancellor Hutchins' insistence on the primary importance of the reading of the world's great books to elaborate schemes for dovetailing courses in the humanities and the sciences.

What I am concerned with is the definition of the educated man which is again emerging. He is, in the language of that same Harvard report, the man who can so reconcile the sense of pattern and direction deriving from heritage with the sense of experiment and innovation deriving from science, that they may exist fruitfully together. That is to say, the educated man has as an integral part of his outlook upon life, the kind of understanding of the tested truths of the ages, and commitment to them, that shall enable him unfailingly to discern value and meaning in the strange process of change in which he finds himself involved; indeed, to find in the manifold circumstances of life, in the course of events, in all that scientific discovery makes known, that which deepens, enlarges, enriches his understanding of these fundamental truths.

Along the same lines, the last report of the Carnegie Foundation, in language which I shall try to translate (for the educational world has its own peculiar jargon), speaks of the way in which in the world of knowledge a few great ideas manifest themselves in countless different forms, and understanding in any given instance means the ability to perceive the essential idea that lies permanently beneath. So, for example, with all its limitations the idea of evolution has served, in any intelligent use of it, to unify great and varied fields of investigation, while for any depth of thinking, it demands some more embracing principle under which it may be subsumed.

If, then, the educated man is one who is able to see life constantly in the light of certain great truths which are of such a kind as to give some knowledge of the permanent reality beneath the changing appearance of things, while yet the very process of change and the infinite variety to which it gives birth bring deeper understanding of that constant reality, ought not the Christian clergyman to take his place once more as, at any rate, one of the educated members of the community? For the Christian faith provides just such a body of fundamental truths. We hold, of course, that this is true in what we are apt to think of as the realm of religion. The basic convictions upon which our worship depends, by which the conduct of our lives and the lives of our people are to be guided, are summed up supremely in the great sentences of the Christian creed. And it is true, as it is increasingly recognized in these days, that the full depth of meaning given in that creed can be entered into only through membership in the fellowship of the Body of Christ since its truths find their complete exposition in the life of the Church.

Unfortunately, along with this altogether right emphasis there goes too often a narrowing of the field of interest. We lost sight of the fact that our creed has its tremendous meaning for life within the Church just because it is nothing less than a philosophy of the whole of life, that it offers nothing less than an interpretation of the universe. The God of whom it speaks is the Maker of heaven and earth, and of all things visible and invisible. It would mean so much if we could continuously think of everything that follows in the creed as revealing the nature of that ultimate reality of personal Being upon whom the whole of existence ceaselessly depends, of God, who in his wisdom and his love exercises everlasting Lordship over every part of the world that he has made, who is *there,* the unfailing constant, the all glorious reality, answering the craving, conscious or unconscious, of every human soul.

> Change and decay in all around I see;
> O thou who changest not, abide with me.

But he is not only there. He is *here* within this process of time, which is no longer, therefore, merely change and decay, *here* by virtue of the moment-by-moment forth-putting of his creative energy, and then supremely *here* in the Incarnation making the whole of human experience his own, the joy and

the sorrow of the world, so that the time process is invested
with eternal significance as it issues at last in the life of the
world to come, a life that shall take up and include forever
all that human hope and aspiration and effort at its best has
done and sought to do.

The Harvard report to which I refer acknowledges this,
as it were, wistfully, because it cannot envisage religious instruction as part of the curriculum.

Historical Christianity has been expressly and consistently concerned
with the importance of this life on earth. The doctrine of the Incarnation, that God took the form of man and inhabited the earth, declares
this concern. While perhaps for Greek thought, only the timeless
realm had importance, in Christian thought the process of history is
vested with absolute significance.

And then it goes on to say,

If the ideal of democracy was rightly described above in the interwoven ideas of the dignity of man (that is, his existence as an independent moral agent) and his duty to his fellow men (that is, his
testing by outward performance), the debt of these two ideas to the
similarly interwoven commandments of the love of God and the love
of neighbor is obvious.

If, then, it be true that at the heart of the problem of education lies the need of reconciling fruitfully what the experience of the ages has shown to be of unchanging value, with
the open-minded acceptance of that which observation and
experiment are constantly bringing to light, we shall do well
to think often of how wonderfully Christian teaching about
God does indeed find room and place for both permanence and
process. Jesus Christ the same yesterday, today, and forever
—and not with the immobility of a timeless abstraction or of
a Platonic idea, but with the warm living identity of personal
being, revealing a God whose love is constantly declared
through every change of circumstance, while the very change
reveals ever new depths and richness in that love, even setting
at the very heart of the world's evil the triumphant sign of the

Cross. It is, perhaps, the most significant philosopher of our own day who has said, "That religion will conquer which can render clear to popular understanding some eternal greatness in the passage of temporal fact."

Thus, attempting to see life steadily and see it whole in the light of the Christian creed, the clergyman may once again regain spiritual leadership in the community, not because he has a ready answer to all the problems political and economic that press so heavily for solution, but because he helps people to see these problems in the light of great fundamental principles, because he has a firm hold upon the values that time has vindicated, right reason, truth, honesty, the sacredness of the individual, the worth of the corporate life, and holds these not as unchanging abstractions but as ways in which the living God declares his will. So there will be a fearless facing of the new situation, a readiness to look for the new ways in which these values may find expression in this life of man. There is that which can kindle men's hearts even in these days of turbulent confusion and disillusionment to new hope, new aspiration, new belief in what life's possibilities may be for every man, in the knowledge of a God who in love is ever making all things new.

You will forgive me, if, being what I am, an ingrained Old Testament man, I conclude with a familiar quotation: "The fear of the Lord," the reverent recognition of the reality of God, "is the beginning of wisdom." If that be true, surely the Christian clergyman may prove himself a really educated man if he will think through all the implications of his creed as it gives the clue to the understanding of the whole of life.

PROPHECY IN REVELATION

❧ I

A band of prophets coming down from the local sanctuary to the accompaniment of lutes, timbrels, flutes, and lyres and responding to this abundant musical stimulus with ecstatic cries—that is the picture given in the well known story of Samuel and Saul (I Sam. 10:5f.), and with it the history of Old Testament prophecy must always begin. The ecstasy of these prophets has so contagious an effect that Saul is caught by it and associates himself with them in their prophesying. The meaning of the verb "prophesy" as denoting the behavior of those who are beside themselves is clearly shown by its use later to describe Saul's ravings at the time that he rewarded David's effort to soothe him with music by threatening him with his spear (I Sam. 18:10 "an evil spirit from God came mightily upon Saul, and he prophesied in the midst of the house." A very late legend pictures a still more striking effect of contact with the prophets: "Saul stripped off his clothes . . . and lay down naked all that day and all that night" (I Sam. 19:24).

The orgiastic nature of primitive prophecy has, of course, long been recognized, though it would seem that English speaking scholarship has only reluctantly come to such recognition. A. B. Davidson, for example, one of the early masters of Old Testament criticism, spoke of "the exercises in which the prophets were engaged" as "probably consisting of singing or other expressions of religious thoughts, accompanied with much fervour or even excitation of manner," a rather staid description of the behavior of dervishes. In recent years, however, the affinity of prophetic ecstasy with similar phenomena in other religions has been more closely studied. An Egyptian papyrus shows the existence of such prophecy at Byblos, a Phoenician city on the coast of Canaan, in the eleventh century B.C., a significant fact in view of the appearance of the prophets of the Phoenician Baal in the Elijah stories. These "leaped about the altar" and "cut themselves after their manner with knives and lances till the blood gushed out upon them" (I Kings 18:25 ff.).

There are frequent references to the same phenomenon in classical and post-classical literature, Herodotus, Aeschylus, Lucian, Apuleius. Significantly enough, these all point to Syria and Asia Minor as the peculiar habitat of this form of religious frenzy. On the other hand, it has become increasingly clear that ecstatic prophecy does not belong to the ancient Semitic world. No traces of it are to be found among the pre-Mohammedan Arabs. Greek writers, so quick to observe the bizarre customs of barbarians, do not appear to have found it in Babylonia. Herodotus speaks of its occurrence in Egypt but insists that it is associated not with native Egyptians but with the Carians from Asia Minor. Islam adopted this strange form of mystic rapture only after Mohammedanism had made itself at home in the regions of the north and east of Arabia. All the evidence of geographical distribution, therefore, suggests that ecstatic prophecy was no part of Israel's desert life but had established itself in Canaan before Israel's entrance into the land and was part of the heritage, religious and cultural, which the nomad tribes appropriated.

More important still is the fact that this type of religious ecstasy was alien to the genius of nomadic Semitic religion. The Semitic mind in its desert setting is characterized by sobriety of thought and by powers of keen observation and practical understanding. It is in the language of today distinctly extrovert. It is deficient in all that inwardness and depth of feeling, that intense emotional susceptibility, that fantasy-breeding power of the imagination, which are important elements in the making of the religious ecstatic. The contrast may fairly be illustrated by reference to two very disparate writers. Doughty in his *Arabia Deserta* remarks that "the sound of the shrilling reed is profane in the Arabs' grave religious bearing. The tambour is the music sound of the religion of Islam." A fragment of Aeschylus touching upon the wild revels of the Dionysos worshipers refers to "the maddening unison" of the deep-toned flute. It will be remembered that Dionysos came to Greece from Thrace, and there was not infrequent migration between Thrace and Asia Minor.

It is of the first importance to note the contrast between the spirit of Yahwism and that of the kind of religious ecstasy which primitive prophecy represented. A rather lengthy passage from Apuleius (*Metamorphisis* VIII, 24-29) may help to bring this out. Lucius, the hero, transformed into an ass as the result of his dabbling in magic has been purchased by a priest of the Syrian goddess and has become part of a strange company.

The day following I saw them apparelled in divers colors, and hideously tricked out, having their faces ruddled with paint, and their eyes tricked out with grease, mitres on their heads, vestments colored like saffron, surplices of silk and linen; and some wore white tunics painted with purple stripes that pointed every way like spears, girt with belts, and on their feet were yellow shoes; and they attired the goddess in a silken robe, and put her upon my back. Then they went forth with their arms naked to their shoulders, bearing with them great swords and mighty axes, shouting and dancing like mad persons to the sound of the pipe. After we had passed many small villages, we fortuned to come to a certain rich man's house, where at our first entry they began to howl all out of tune and hurl themselves hither and thither, as though they were mad. They made a thousand gests with their feet and their heads; they would bend down their necks and spin round so that their hair flew out in a circle; they would bite their own flesh; finally, everyone took his two-edged weapon and wounded his arms in divers places. Meanwhile, there was one more mad than the rest, that fetched many deep sighs from the bottom of his heart, as though he had been ravished in spirit, or replenished with divine power, and he feigned a swoon and frenzy, as if, forsooth, the presence of the gods were not wont to make men better than before, but weak and sickly.

This is the account given by a satirist who rightly insists on the mercenary motive behind the performance but perhaps makes too much of the note of pretence. Of particular interest for our purpose is the frantic dancing to the sound of the pipe, the howling and the shouting, the self-wounding, and, especially significant, the conduct of the man who feigned a swoon, not only because of the parallel with Saul lying "naked all that day and all that night" but because it is clear that the swooning was one of the ways in which the mystic rapture could find its complete fulfillment.

It may be worth while to draw also upon Rohde's penetrating analysis of the mood of the Dionysos worshipers.

The worshipers, too, in furious exaltation and divine inspiration, strive after the god; they seek communion with him. They burst the physical barriers of their soul. A magic power takes hold of them; they feel themselves raised high above the level of their everyday existence; they seem to *become* those spiritual beings who wildly dance in the train of the god. Nay, more, they have a share in the life of the god himself; nothing less can be the meaning of the fact that the enraptured servants of the god call themselves by the name of the god. (*Psyche,* p. 258)

Now it is, of course, true that in its desert days Israel had had its own experience of possession. The wild exultation of the battle frenzy speaks clearly through such a poem as the Song of Deborah. The power of the dread storm-god seized upon the warriors, lifted them to new levels of achievement as, careless of what might befall them, they hurled themselves upon the foe. A passage in the book of Amos puts in significant parallelism the prophets and the Nazarites, originally, dedicated long-haired warriors. "And I raised up of your sons for prophets, and of your young men for Nazarites" (Amos 2:11).

But this fighting rapture differed from other forms of primitive ecstasy in three important respects. First, there was always about Yahweh's coming in power an element of the incalculable. It was as unpredictable as the advent of storm or earthquake, but the ecstasy of the prophets could be induced by a definite technique of music, dance, and other forms of rhythmic movement. The presence of deity could be compelled from the human side, whereas in Yahwism the initiative lay with God and not with man. The spirit of Yahweh leapt suddenly and unexpectedly upon Samson, and he rent the lion as he would have rent a kid (Judges 14:6). In the second place, in Yahwism the energy that seized upon men used them for ends beyond themselves. They became the instruments of the power that laid hold of them. Their activity was directed outwards and issued in such definitely practical achievement as that represented by fighting in battle. Nor was fighting the only outlet for the heightened sense of power. Late, but thoroughly in keeping with the genius of primitive Yahwism, is the account of Bezalel ben Uri, one of the artificers of the tabernacle, "See, Yahweh hath called (him) by name . . . and he hath filled him with the spirit of God, in wisdom, in understanding, and in knowledge, and in all manner of workmanship" (Exodus 35:30-31). In the non-Israelite ecstasy, however, the energy was directed inwards. The recipients became as it were the containers rather than the instruments of the divine energy. The enlargement and extension of one's own being was an end in itself. The experience of possession by deity was sought for its own sake. Psychologically, as well as in other respects, there is a world of difference between activity which issues in the rending of a lion and that which finds an outlet in wounding one's self. It is not fanciful to see, in the prostrate swooning figure of a man sunk in cataleptic trance, or in the howling dervish achieving complete revolution round his own axis, fitting symbols of two different ways in which religious introversion can reach its climax.

Sometimes, to be sure, the abnormal visionary or auditory experience which could thus be induced could be regarded as forecasting the future; the ravings could become in part intelligible, or could be interpreted as if they were, and considered to have predictive value. But what thus found expression was simply a dominant wish of the group. "Go up to Ramoth Gilead and prosper," said the four hundred prophets to Ahab (I Kings 22:12). "They speak a vision of their own heart," says the book of Jeremiah (23:16). Ecstasy meant not an escape from self, but imprisonment within the circle of one's own desires.

In the third place, what is sought in ecstasy is actual identification with the life of the god. The worshipers in their frenzied exaltation seem to become one with deity. They are *entheoi,* god-indwelt. This is abundantly clear in the case of the Dionysos cult in Greece and its antecedents in Thrace. As Rohde points out, "the enraptured servants of the god call themselves by the name of the god." The worshipers of Bacchus are Bacchae. Now the prophetic bands of the Old Testament are seen only as they are in process of being transformed by Yahwism. But effects of older beliefs persist. In the incident to which reference has already been made, Zedekiah ben Chenaanah made him horns of iron and said, "Thus saith Yahweh, With these shalt thou push the Syrians until they be consumed" (I Kings 22:11). He is playing the role of the bull-god. So participants in the Bacchus festival set horns upon their heads. The distinctive dress of the prophet was the hairy mantle, originally perhaps the hide of the bull. The enthusiasts express their sense of identification with the god by assuming as far as possible his appearance. Now this belief in the fusion of the human and the divine rests upon a conception of the relation between god and man entirely foreign to Yahwism. In this the distinction between the two was from the beginning so absolute as to forbid the suggestion that even for a moment a human being could live the life of divinity. It is the spirit of Yahweh, not Yahweh himself, that comes upon Saul and joins him to the prophets' god-given power but not the being of God himself.

On these grounds, then, as on the grounds of geographical distinction, it becomes increasingly clear that primitive prophetism (1) with its self-initiated effort, (2) to take possession of deity, (3) for its own enjoyment, was not a native product of Israel's religion but, like much else in Canaan, was taken over by Yahwism and radically transformed. It is, indeed, a far cry from the bands of ecstatics to the great solitary figure of a Hosea, a Micah, or a Jeremiah; from the hardly intelligible ravings of enthusiasts to the terrible clarity of an Amos or an Isaiah; from the devotees who have found a refuge from the actual in the vaporings of their own excited fantasy to the men who have accepted fearlessly the dread impact of austere reality. One of the things which has not been accounted for by those who would make the distinctive character of Israel's religion begin with the eighth-century prophets is the extraordinary dynamic needed to effect this transformation of ecstatic prophetism into the later prophecy. Yet, along with this remarkable change, certain characteristics of the older prophetism persisted in the ministry of the later prophets, and the recognition of these characteristics as giving form to their utterances has a very definite bearing upon the interpretation of the books that bear their names.

The visions of an Isaiah or an Amos are evidently born of ecstatic experience. Amos, for example, sees a basket of summer fruit (Amos 8:1-2). He finds himself fixedly gazing at it. In his inner consciousness there sounds a voice, "Amos, what seest thou?" There is here something more than meets the eye. In Hebrew the word for "summer fruit" closely resembles that for "end," and to a heart charged with the sense of impending doom such a word has an ominous ring. There breaks upon his inner hearing the solemn pronouncement, "The end is come upon my people Israel." This suggestibility resulting in the trance-like condition is that of the ecstatic. Again abnormal powers of sight and hearing, an intense emotional impressionability, the sense of inner compulsion— "Yahweh spake thus to me with a strong hand" (Is. 8:11)— alike reveal the kinship of the great prophets with the earlier dervish-like companies. Jeremiah announcing the coming of the invader cries, "How long must I see the standard and hear the sound of the trumpet?" (4:21) His imagination is aflame with vivid anticipation of the terrors that are to come. There is a direct response to stimulus, and the expression of that response is immediate and unreflecting. The prophet speaks of things seen and heard and felt. The accents are those of the living voice. Very different are passages which are the result of literary effort. Take the following from the book of Amos:

> Yahweh roars from Zion,
> And utters his voice from Jerusalem;
> And the pastures of the shepherds mourn,
> And the ridge of Carmel withers. (1:2)

The passage is in part to be found also in Joel (3:16); the reference to Jerusalem suggests that if God declares himself, there will be some association with the Holy City; the shepherd of Tekoa must speak, as it were, in the name of the Church. For these reasons it is unlikely that the passage can be taken as coming from Amos himself. But it is almost as important to note that the imagery is confused. The first half of the verse uses the roaring of the lion and the thunder as symbols of God's majesty and power, but neither of these would produce the drought of which the second half of the verse speaks. The writer has not heard or felt these things. The language is conventional. Contrast with this Amos's own use of similar imagery:

> The lion roars,
> Who does not shudder?
> Yahweh speaks,
> Who can help prophesying? (3:8)

A second notable sign of the ecstatic background of prophecy is the use of the pronoun of the first person singular for the divine utterance upon the prophet's lips.

> Disaster do I bring from the north,
> And a great destruction. (Jer. 4:6)

> To what purpose unto me the multitude
> of your sacrifices? (Is. 1:11)

God himself speaks through the prophet. It is the word of the Lord that has taken possession of the man. The experience of union is both like and unlike that of the earlier ecstatic. It is not a fusion of the human and the divine which loses all consciousness of anything but the sense of its own heightened existence. The prophet is a mediator between God and the world, the vehicle through which the dynamic word passes on to human life. As the initiative is not with a man's self but with Yahweh, so the end is beyond self. But the capacity for surrender has its very evident relationship to the intense emotional susceptibility of the ecstatic, though with the prophet this surrender is not to a nature deity with its cyclic manifestation but to the will of a righteous Being who declares himself in history as well as in nature. The full significance of this astounding phenomenon is hardly realized by the ordinary reader. It is assumed that the prophet is simply reporting verbatim a message previously conveyed to him. Color is lent to this interpretation by the prefatory formula, "Thus saith the Lord," which perhaps should be better rendered, "Thus did the Lord say." The clause is generally the contribution of those who have transmitted to us in writing the oracles of the prophets. For the original hearers there was no need of such an introductory statement. There was that about the look and bearing of the prophet, and the content of his message, which made it abundantly clear that another than himself was speaking. What men felt as they listened was the actual presence and power of the living God. Prophetic utterance is not, of course, always phrased in this way. The prophets often speak of God in the third person. Again, there are passages in which the use of the pronoun "I" as of God is a writer's way of acknowledging his indebtedness to inspiration, and these passages have often very great value even if the use be derivative. But the deeper understanding of the prophets will always depend on the recapturing of the accents of the living voice. For example, there is a well-known passage in Isaiah (3:13-15):

> Yahweh is set to contend,
> And standeth to judge his people
> Yahweh entereth into judgment
> With the elders of his people, and their princes.

Thus far we have the setting of the stage and the enunciation of a truth, important and sublime, though set forth with a certain repetition to meet the demands of the verse-form. But there is a distinct change in tone in what follows as God himself speaks:

> 'Tis ye that have devoured the vineyard;
> The spoil of the poor is in your houses.
> What mean ye that ye crush my people,
> And grind the faces of the poor?

That is the bitter challenge which is hurled in the teeth of the rich, and they who hear it know full well that the burning indignation is that of the great God himself. The explanatory introduction is for the later reader.

In the third place, the language of ecstasy is generally rhythmic, and the prophet as poet derives from the same source. It is well to keep this in mind because the idea is sometimes advanced that the poetic form of prophetic utterance is the result of the literary elaboration of their thought. It cannot be denied that poems of some length in which the development of an idea is the main feature are to be found in the books of the prophets, but by that very token these are of later origin and stand in striking contrast to the pregnant spontaneity of the authentic oracles. A striking illustration may be found in the second chapter of the book of Jeremiah. Imbedded in the opening verses is a poem of characteristic tenderness:

> I remember the kindness of thy youth,
> The love of thine espousals,
> How thou wentest after me in the wilderness,
> A land not sown.
> Holy unto Yahweh was Israel,
> The first fruits of his increase:
> All that would devour it stood guilty;
> Disaster o'ertook them. (2:2f.)

Even in the translation the rhythm is unmistakable, three thought-units followed by two. The rhythm recurs again in the fourteenth and fifteenth verses:

> [And now] Israel a slave,
> A house-born serf,
> Wherefore hath he become a prey,
> His cities burned?
> Against him young lions roar,
> Give forth their voice;
> They have made his land a waste
> Without inhabitant. (2:14)

The theme is a simple one, the pitiful contrast of then and now, the days when Israel walked in loving loyalty with Yahweh, sheltered from harm amid the perils of the wilderness, and the present desolation of a people that have forgotten their God. But between the parts of this poem there is a long passage which halts between prose and poetry, for while it has a certain rhythmic swing, no regularity of the rhythm can be discerned. It is too long to quote in its entirety, but some verses will suffice to make it clear that the theme is the same of that of the poem.

What unrighteousness have your fathers found in me, that they are gone far from me, and have walked after vanity, and are become vain? Neither said they, Where is Yahweh that brought us up out of the land of Egypt, that led us through the wilderness, through a land of deserts and of pits, through a land of drought and of thick darkness, through a land that none passed through, and where no man dwelt? (2:5-6

Be astonished, O ye heavens, at this, and be horribly afraid, be ye very desolate, saith Yahweh. For my people have committed two evils; they have forsaken me the fountain of living waters, and hewed them out cisterns, broken cisterns, that can hold no water. (2:12-13)

The changes are rung effectively on the baseness and the folly of a people's forsaking their God, who has done so much for them. The author enforces his point with moving eloquence, but his style is that of the preacher rather than the poet. The treatment of the desert by the two writers is significant. The poet is content with the single revealing epithet, "a land not sown," but that epithet seizes at once the essential feature of the desert, its oblivion of human effort, a land where none would ever speak of Mother Earth and man remains a stranger and a wanderer. (It is interesting to see the phrase recurring more than once in T. E. Lawrence's *Pillars of Wisdom*.) "The wilderness," says the prose writer, "a land of deserts and of pits, a land of drought and of thick darkness, a land that none passed through and where no man dwelt." This method of enumeration has its own rhetorical adequacy, but it does not give the feel of the desert as the poet's single phrase does. The difference in tone and style and language of the prose passage—for its vocabulary echoes that of the Deuteronomic editors of the book—justifies German scholars in their contention that it is not from Jeremiah himself. Indeed, it reads very much like a sermon based, as it were, upon the poem for its text.*

* Splendid is the conclusion: the contrast between the fountain of living waters and the cisterns which men hew out for themselves; the inexhaustible giving of God and the very limited resources on which they draw who depend

The conclusion, then, to which a just appreciation of the ecstatic element in prophecy leads is this. The prophets themselves did not compose speeches or even poems in which they developed a theme with some degree of logical consistency. Their utterances were brief, pregnant oracles, charged with an emotional intensity which found expression in a rhythmic form, probably maintained unbroken through any particular deliverance. That is to say, change in rhythm, in mood, in imagery, is a likely indication that a new oracle is to be reckoned with. Often, too, these changes will be found to coincide with the occurrence of the introductory formula, "Thus did the Lord say," or the concluding phrase, "saith Yahweh"; and it would seem likely that editors have thus preserved the tradition of separate origin. Some of these oracles may have been afterwards committed to writing by the prophet himself. This is certainly true in the case of Isaiah (see 30:8). Jeremiah dictated his poems to Baruch. But, for the most part, they would have lived in the memories of hearers who, in the course of time, recorded them on ostraca, parchment, or whatever materials were available. Such fragmentary records, for the most part associated with a significant name, would be cherished and, no doubt, copied and recopied. A man into whose possession a small collection of these oracles came would take delight in adding to it other utterances reputed to be by the same author, and he would not question too curiously their source. Enough that the words rang true. Superimposed upon this process of informal growth was the work of those who, feeling that the oracles were of timeless value, sought to relate them to the conditions of their own day and age, adding, therefore, interpretation, explanation, commentary, and even qualification. Often they felt themselves so much under the spell

---

only on their own efforts. Very effective is the further statement that in the end these cisterns are broken and hold no water; but men do not thus "hew them out"; and it may be asked whether there is not here a touch of the rhetoric which sometimes betrays the preacher into a departure from his main theme.

of the utterances which lay before them that they identified themselves with the prophet and believed that they were empowered and guided by the spirit that had spoken through him. Their work may be regarded as the result of a kind of mediated inspiration, but it is significant that many telling passages in the books of the prophets derive from such a source (e.g., Nahum 1). Indeed, it may fairly be questioned whether the prophets could ever have counted as they have in the life of a people and of the race, without the devoted labors of these many nameless disciples. To no one man, not even to the greatest of the prophets, is it given to see the whole of God's revelation of himself. There is a splendid one-sidedness about the prophet that is part of his unhesitating loyalty to the truth of his own immediate vision. That one-sidedness is, in no small measure, made part of a larger understanding of God's way with man by the work of those through whose labors the prophet's utterances have been transmitted. Dr. Streeter has recently remarked that "the Bible itself is a monument of the principle that the validity of individual intuitions must be checked by the conscience and insight of the religious community." That principle finds pre-eminent expression in the growth of the books of the prophets.

It is, then, an immensely fruitful task in which criticism is engaged, that of distinguishing between the prophet and his book, fruitful because the prophet, meaning by the word an Isaiah, an Amos, a Jeremiah, emerges with clearer definition in all his singleness of mind and his solitary grandeur, while at the same time, released from the necessity of explaining all that is included in the book as coming from the same source, the critic is free to do justice to the contributions made by others in the light of their purpose and intention, and of the particular needs they sought to meet. An interesting illustration of this is Bernhard Duhm's commentary on the book of Jeremiah, a work to which unfortunately there is nothing corresponding in English. It may be that Duhm has used his criteria too rigorously, for he regards as genuine utterances of Jeremiah only two hundred and sixty-eight couplets, all of the same rhythmic form. But it is certain that, through the consideration of these, the figure of the prophet emerges with singular distinction in all his heroic tenderness. The defect of Duhm's work lies in his practical refusal to admit genuine worth in the secondary material. There is need of commentaries which will combine with a power of penetrating analysis and sympathetic understanding of the prophet's heart a like sympathy in interpreting the work of the preachers and editors through whom the prophet's vision was made meaningful for succeeding generations.

≥ II

When the distinction between the prophet and his book has been fairly recognized and the consequences of that distinction for the interpretation of prophecy have been accepted, one arresting truth stands out with clearer decisiveness than before. In their ministry, Amos, Hosea, Micah, Isaiah, Jeremiah, and Ezekiel, all alike foretell the final doom that is to overtake the nation. "Yahweh is about to destroy Israel for its sins," might well be taken as a summary of the message of every one of them. Any attempt to understand the distinctive greatness of these men must therefore reckon with the way in which this apparent pessimism dominates their ministry.

The mysterious opening sentence of each of the oracles placed at the beginning of the book of Amos strikes an unmistakable note: For three transgressions of Damascus, of the children of Ammon, of Moab, of Israel, and for four, "I will not turn it back." Turn what back? The desolating disaster, with a foreboding sense of which the prophet's heart is filled. It is as if he long had brooded over the question, Cannot this terrible doom which threatens my world be averted? Is it inevitable? And always there beats in his brain with monotonous insistence the sound of the voice of Another than himself, "I will not turn it back. I will not withhold my hand." Yahweh himself, on the lips of the prophet, thus declares his irrevocable purpose to destroy. Is there then nothing to be saved out of the wreckage of which he speaks? With bitter irony the herdsman of Tekoa replies:

> The shepherd rescues from the lion's mouth
> A pair of legs or a bit of an ear, (Amos 3:12)

the worthless remnants, good only to show that the animal has actually been destroyed by a wild beast. So the children of Israel shall be delivered.

Popular religion of the day speaks of the coming of "the day of Yahweh," the day when their God shall declare himself in all his majesty and power for the exaltation of his chosen people, and Amos taunts his hearers:

> Woe unto you that desire the day of Yahweh!
> What's it to you? Yahweh's day,
> Is it not darkness, and no light?
> Thick darkness with no brightness in it? (5:18, 20)

He represents—and the word is to be taken literally—Yahweh as coming in death-dealing judgment.

> In all vineyards wailing:
> For I pass through thy midst. (5:17)

And there is a terrible simplicity about the prophet's dirge over his people.

> Fallen never to stand again
> Virgin of Israel;
> Prostrate she lies on her own land,
> With none to raise her. (5:2)

So he sees the chill immobility of death fasten upon a nation in the prime of youth.

A consideration of the four visions (7:1-9; 8:1-3) which really constituted part of the experience through which the prophet was called to his ministry points unhesitatingly to the same conclusion. Locusts and drought seem to him to threaten the land, but as he finds himself praying for his people, he comes to feel that the danger is averted and he dares to hope. But there follow two more visions, that of the plumb-line and that of the basket of summer fruit, and an awful certainty seizes him. There can be no further hope of forgiveness.

> The end is come upon my people Israel;
> I will not pass by them any more. (8:2)

It was under the compulsion of that dread certainty that Amos became a prophet.

The book also includes a fragment of biography, and here again the gist of the prophet's message is clear enough. Amaziah the priest sums it up, "Israel shall surely be led away captive out of his land" (7:11).

Very simple and closely akin to that of Amos is the burden of Hosea's message. The end is at hand, Israel must be destroyed. Her sins have brought the nation to ruin. The national career is run. There is no future. God has doomed Israel to final destruction.

> Ephraim, desolation shall he become
> In the day of chastisement:
> Concerning the tribes of Israel
> Do I make known that which shall surely be. (5:9)

> > The days of visitation are come,
> > The days of recompense are here. (9:7)

There is a strange vehemence about the divine indignation. By comparison the wrath of the God of Amos seems stern and passionless. With him was struck a note that suggests what,

at times, seems to be nature's inflexible contempt for man, as
she simply blots him out.

> Powers that never measured the earth
> Of bird or beast or soul.

With Amos it might almost be said that Yahweh destroys as
one to whom destruction is a natural and inevitable activity.
Not so with the God of Hosea. The divine effort makes itself
felt. God must urge himself on, as it were, against his will.
Now and again this imparts a certain savagery into the pronouncement of doom.

> I will be to them as the lion:
> As a leopard by the way will I lie in wait.
> I will attack them as a bear bereaved of her whelps,
> And will rend the caul of their hearts. (Hos. 13:7-8)

The enraged animal standing over the prey and tearing at its
vitals is bold imagery for the depiction of God in action.
Again God speaks through the prophet:

> Woe unto them that they have departed from me!
> Destruction to them that they have been untrue to me! (7:13)

And once more in the familiar passage:

> From the power of Sheol shall I ransom them;
> From death shall I redeem them:
> Where are thy plagues, O death?
> Where thy destruction, O Sheol? (13:14).

Whatever the difficulty of translation and interpretation of
these lines, that which follows, "Repentance is hid from mine
eyes," has no note of ambiguity about it but speaks with terrible finality.

Limitations of time forbid dealing with the other prophets
at the same length. In the case of Micah it must be sufficient
to quote what is now by many scholars regarded as the conclusion of his prophecy:

> Because of you Zion shall be plowed as a field,
> Jerusalem be heaps,
> The mount of the house become
> A jungle mound. (Mic. 3:12)

The account of Isaiah's inaugural vision bears ample testimony to the general character of his message. He is to exercise what has been called a ministry of hardening, that is to say, the impact of his message upon his people is to reveal the justice of the doom that is to overtake them.

Go tell this people, Hear ye indeed, but understand not; and see ye indeed, but perceive not. Make the heart of this people fat, and make their ears heavy, and shut their eyes; lest they see with their eyes, and hear with their ears, and understand with their heart, and be healed again. (Is. 6:9, 10)

And he is to carry on this ministry "until cities be waste without inhabitant and houses without man and the land become utterly waste" (6:11). And what is generally admitted to be Isaiah's last word to his people is this:

> Yahweh of hosts hath revealed himself in mine ears,
> Surely this iniquity shall not be purged from you
>   till ye die. (22:14)

Jeremiah's agonized preoccupation with the destruction that is to come upon the nation and his fearless proclamation of the inevitable end at a time when all the national forces were being rallied for the last death struggle align him with his great predecessors of the eighth century. His contemporary Ezekiel, viewing the struggle from far-off Babylonia, repeats with almost inhuman exultation, "An end is come, the end is come." (7:6)

There can be no question, then, of the central place which the announcement of doom takes in the ministry of these prophets. But is their message an unqualified prediction of woe? Do they not envisage a recovery of the nation after the divine visitation? In the books as we have them there are passages which speak of this, notably at the end of the books or at the end of the smaller collections of oracles of which the books are composed, but there is quite general agreement among scholars that these prophecies of restoration come from others than the reputed authors of the books. From this decision there are hardly any dissenting voices in the case of Amos and Micah. But there is division of opinion about Hosea. The story of his relations with his wife, as they are set forth in the first three chapters, gives rise to many questions. But when it is noted that the restoration of Hosea's wife is by no means explicitly stated and that the third chapter, in which it is implied, is distinctly allegorical in tone—when, too, the approach to the consideration of these chapters is made as it ought to be through the main body of the oracles given in chapters 4—14, which consist almost entirely of invective against Israel's sin and proclamation of doom—there is substantial reason for holding that Hosea himself knew nothing of such a possibility of restoration. It was later writers who felt the intensity of Hosea's portrayal of the love of God and rightly believed that in the end such love could not be defeated and that therefore forgiveness must follow, God's forgiveness of his people and then Hosea's forgiveness of his wife. At any rate, George Adam Smith, who contends valiantly for the authenticity and historical character of the narrative in question, is nonetheless compelled to say, "I think it extremely likely that Hosea's ministry closed with that final hopeless proclamation in Chapter 13:16: "Samaria must bear her guilt, for she hath rebelled against her God."

A word must be said about what is known as Isaiah's doctrine of the Remnant, that the future lay with the faithful few who should survive the downfall of the nation and should be the instrument through which God's work would be continued among his people. Of the importance of this doctrine in later times it is not the place to speak here. It must suffice to note the very minor role which it plays in the prophet's recorded utterances. Here again, his last word, to which reference has already been made, must be kept in mind as bringing to final expression the same sense of irrevocable doom with which his ministry began. "Surely this iniquity shall not be purged from you till ye die."

Thus far, then, these prophets seem to have no hope for the future of their people. But another possibility must be considered. Was there not in their hearts the expectation that the nation might repent, and thus the final catastrophe be averted? Did not this hope sustain them in their appallingly difficult ministry? The prophets are often described as preachers of repentance, and moving exhortations to the people to turn from their evil ways are to be found in their books. If the predictions of doom are absolute, and disaster is inevitable, then a certain unreality attaches to these exhortations. Repentance could not avert the catastrophe. If, on the other hand, the call to repentance is to be taken seriously and there is a possibility that it will produce an effect, then it is exceedingly difficult to explain the unhesitating certainty with which the prophets declare that the fate of the nation is sealed. The dilemma is ably stated by Dr. Skinner in his *Prophecy and Religion* (pp. 74ff.), but the compromise at which he arrives leaves the problem much where it was. When, however, due account is taken of the trenchant brevity of the oracles, and it is further noted that introductory formulas and change of rhythm or of imagery mark in many cases the exhortations as separate and distinct utterances, it seems at least very probable that these have been added to the original oracles of doom by those who sought to relate the prophet's revelation of God more definitely to human needs, teachers for whom, too, the distinctions within the nation which have their roots in Isaiah's ministry had become a basic postulate. An interesting illustration is to be found in the fifth chapter of the book of Amos. In the midst of invective and predictions of woe there is a powerful appeal to the moral consciousness. Part of it runs as follows:

Seek good, and not evil, that ye may live:
And so shall Yahweh of hosts be with you, as ye say.
Hate the evil, and love the good; and set up justice
    in the gate:
It may be that Yahweh the God of hosts will be
    gracious unto the remnant of Joseph. (Amos 5:14-15)

The reference to the remnant of Joseph points at once to a later date than that of Amos. The "maybe" is quite out of keeping with the categorical note which characterizes the prophet's utterances generally. George Adam Smith takes the verses as a parenthesis, but "whether," he says, "from Amos himself or from a later writer, who can tell?" And he adds, "But it ought to be kept in mind that in other prophetic writing where judgment is very severe, we have some proof of the later insertion of calls to repentance by way of mitigation." The principle is of wider application than is as yet generally recognized. But let it be said at once that to say this does not mean that the passage in question is robbed of its significance. It is simply to distinguish between the task committed to the prophet of setting forth unfalteringly the inexorable nature of the divine righteousness and that of another who taking home to his heart the truth enunciated by Amos draws out more richly its bearing upon human living.

This means that prediction was of the essence of their ministry. They knew what God was about to do. It is important to keep this in mind for it has almost become orthodox criticism to minimize the predictive element. The Brown-Driver-Briggs Hebrew Lexicon, for example, elaborates the meaning of the Hebrew verb "prophesy" as follows: "in oldest forms, religious ecstasy with or without song and music; later, essentially religious instruction, with occasional prediction." It is true that the prophets were not, as was once thought, concerned with forecasting future events, more or less remote. Ewald's canon holds, "Every genuine prophetic word proceeded from its own age and was primarily intended for it." "Forthteller" is perhaps a better word than "foreteller" to describe the prophet. He is the interpreter of the will of God, but it is always to be remembered that that will is not an ideal laid up in the heavens but power revealing itself in unceasing energy within the world and in impact upon it. To interpret the divine will is to interpret the divine activity. That means the setting forth of what God is going to do.

These prophets then know that God is going to destroy. Whence comes this certainty? Any attempt at explanation must acknowledge that complete rationalization of the phenomenon is impossible. At best there can be discerned only some of the factors that contributed to their conviction. One of these was, undoubtedly, the sense of God's destroying power bound up with the primitive conception of Yahweh, the Sinai God. The storm-god was pre-eminently the destroyer. In battle, in surrender to that demonic energy which made itself felt in the tempest, Israel had known what it was to be the instrument of the divine wrath. An oracle of Isaiah's manifestly echoes this primitive experience:

Ho! Ashur, rod of mine anger,
Staff of mine indignation.
Against a profane nation do I send him,
Against the people of my wrath do I give him a charge,
To take the spoil and to take the prey,
And tread them down like the mire in the streets. (10:5)

The formidable Assyrian power advancing with irresistible might is God's chosen instrument. Assyria is playing the part that once had been Israel's fearful privilege, but the divine anger is now turned against that same Israel which has become "a profane people," the people upon whom God's wrath is to be poured out. And there is about Isaiah's utterance a note almost of exultation, as of an identification with the divine will to destroy, not unlike the ecstatic surrender in warfare of Israel's nomad life.

It is true that in the centuries that had elapsed since those nomad days, there had been the work of Moses and all that followed from it. There had been, too, the life in Canaan

from which Israel had learned much. They had come to know
God as not simply a God of power but a God of justice and of
love. But this justice and this love partook of that strange
and awful dynamic which had declared itself from the first.
Feeling this deeply, the prophets were sensitive, as others
were not, to the significance of the disruptive forces in the
world of their day. While their countrymen identified God
with that which made for the well-being and prosperity of the
nation, these rare souls could discern him at work in the
forces which threatened the nation. That was not the whole
truth, but for the moment it was the significant truth. "Prophecies," said Dr. Davidson, "are usually suggested by some
great movement among the nations in which Yahweh's presence is already felt"; and Dr. Skinner, who quotes this, adds,
"The prophet's mind is the seismograph of providence, vibrat-
ing to the first faint tremors that herald the coming earthquake." And it was not only in the catastrophic that this destructive aspect of the divine activity was to be felt. There
is an illuminating oracle of Hosea's:

> I am as the moth to Ephraim,
> As decay to the house of Israel. (5:12)

In the gradual process of dissolution going on within the nation the prophet felt God declaring himself.

In the much debated question, then, as to which is primary
in the prophet's consciousness—the awareness of this inexorable power which threatened the overturn of his world, or
his abhorrence of the sin of his people—there can be little
doubt that the starting point is his sense of God's coming in
power to judgment. So in Isaiah's call it is the divine holiness
that constitutes appalling danger for the man of unclean lips
and for the people of unclean lips among whom he dwells.
When a Micah declares, in contrast to the false prophets:

> But I truly am full of power,
> Of judgment, of might,
> To declare unto Jacob his transgression,
> To Israel his sin (3:8),

he is not so much, as has been said, the incarnate conscience of the nation, as one who has become participant in the divine righteousness; and this righteousness throws into fearful relief the human iniquity which it is about to destroy.

> Is not my word like fire?
> Like a hammer that shatters the rock? (Jer. 23:29)

This is Jeremiah's way of describing God's ingress into life through the prophet.

External evidence to this primary dependence of the great prophets upon their awareness of Yahweh's immanence in destroying power is afforded by the fact that they appear only in time of crisis, as in the last half of the eighth century when the Assyrian empire was demolishing kingdoms or in the beginning of the sixth century when southwestern Asia was again in ferment. From the first half of the seventh century when the Assyrian power prevailed and comparative stability had been reached, no name of a prophet announcing doom has come down, though it was a time when Israel's idolatry was flagrant and its sins grievous, a condition to which the reformation under Josiah bears abundant testimony.

It is worth while thus to insist upon the central significance of these prophets' proclamation of Yahweh's purpose to destroy the nation, because only thus can the unique contribution which they made to the knowledge of God be rightly understood. In the first place, the event justified their prediction, even though in the case of a Micah and an Isaiah the final blow was longer delayed than they had anticipated. The destruction of Jerusalem in 586 *was* the end of Israel's career as a nation. That it persisted as a people, while surrounding nations whom a like fate had befallen gradually lost their identity and ceased to exist as peoples, was owing to the fact that Israel's God was not involved in the final disaster that had overtaken the nation. The prophets had made it clear that in the awful catastrophe it was none other than Yahweh himself who had declared his power and his righteousness.

Israel's survival and the remarkable part it was to play in succeeding centuries derive, in no small degree, from the unfaltering announcement of the prophets that Yahweh would destroy
his own people.

But, in the second place, that stern pronouncement embodied an essential truth about the nature and being of Israel's
God, a truth which was all too easily forgotten. In Canaan
the prevailing type of religion was a nature worship, and the
local gods, the Baalim, were regarded as the bestowers of fertility, givers of corn and wine and oil, ministrants to human
need, finding their own well-being in the prosperity of the
communities which they served. Here was an aspect of the
Divine of great significance, and Yahwism, after Israel had
settled in Canaan, took into itself the truth embodied in this
conception of deity. The belief in God's tender concern for
man as shown in the stories of the patriarchs, even the amazing love of which Hosea speaks, has its source, in part, in this
religion of the land. But as so often in the history of religion,
that which satisfies ordinary human craving had come to dom-
inate, and Yahweh had to all intents and purposes been as-
similated to the Baalim. He was thought of as existing for
man. His power was, of course, far greater than that of the
local deities both in range and intensity, but this very greatness could be regarded as a national asset. All the stern demand that his righteousness makes upon man, all that was
involved in the fearful privilege of being used by him for the
fulfillment of his will had been forgotten. So Amos characterizes the worship at the sanctuaries as the light-hearted satisfaction of men's own desire.

> This is what ye *like* to do,
> Ye children of Israel. (4:5)

Over against this easy appropriation of God he sets the picture of One who has been calling his people to repentance in
famine and drought and pestilence and war and earthquake.

The announcement that God was about to destroy his people for their sins was a solemn assertion of the truth that God was greater than the nation, that man exists for God, not God for man.

But even deeper still, this emphasis on God's power to destroy kept before men an essential factor in the relationship between God and man. The significance of Israel's realizing itself as the chosen instrument of One whose power was manifest in storm and earthquake and volcano is, perhaps, not sufficiently understood. It means that these nomad clans had faced what seemed only the mad fury of the elements, all that seemed to threaten life with extinction, and had found at the heart of all that devastating power that which drew them into union with itself, quickening and enhancing all their energies and lifting them to unlooked-for heights of achievement. The numinous had laid hold of them, and they had been brought out on the other side of fear. It is the kind of experience of which the Song of Deborah speaks. To learn, as they did in process of time, that this same power was revealed in the gradual, kindly processes of nature, that it entered into relation with the everyday concerns of human living, caring for justice as between man and man, that it was righteousness and love, was all part of what Rudolph Otto would call the rationalization of the numinous but might be better described as God's gradual revelation of himself to his people. But human nature being what it is, it could easily be forgotten that behind this revelation lay the elemental mystery of the divine Being, that God cannot be included within any human categories, formulas, or institutions. In a very real sense the prophets were contending for the freedom of God when they proclaimed his power to destroy his own people in vindication of his righteousness and his holy love. He is Lord, always, of his own creation. The bearing of this upon the thought of our day was well put by C. G. Montefiore, the great leader of liberal Judaism, in an article written some years ago.

Man is created in the image of God; there is a kinship between God and man. If God is the source and guarantee of human reason and human righteousness, reason and righteousnes cannot mean one thing in man and an utterly and entirely different thing in God. All this Judaism teaches and allows. But, perhaps, today, with even more emphatic insistence, it declares that God and man are different from each other, and that there was, and is, and will be no man who was not, is not, and will not be infinitely removed from the absolute perfection of the Divine. The servant is other than the Master; the human child will never grow into the complete stature or the perfect likeness of the Divine Father. Today such doctrine seems somewhat unfashionable; we are constantly reminded of the fundamental unity of man's nature with God's. We are almost taught to sneer at those anachronistic persons who "make a distinct cleavage between man and God, and whose inheritance of the exploded Deistic idea of an absolutely transcendent God, blinds them to the immanence of the Divine Life." Judaism, however, is not ashamed to make and to stress "a distinct cleavage between man and God." Man must not be allowed to come too near to the inexhaustible richness of the Divine. Kinship is one thing; essential unity is another. "An absolutely transcendent God;" perhaps not; but a purely immanent God still less. The pantheistic slope is slippery. The God who seems hardly to exist to any purpose except in man seems likely before very long to become a God very far removed from the God of the Psalmists or of Jesus. Once more, Judaism holds aloft its warning. (*Hibbert Journal,* July 1923)

As today the effort is gropingly made to restore a right conception of the transcendence of God, it will increasingly be found that the prophet's truth to his vision of the majesty of God, though a world lie in ruins, has its own indispensable contribution to make.

⇒ III

To speak of the prophet's faithfulness to his vision of the
majesty of God is to touch upon the mystery of his inner personal experience. That must always remain holy ground.
Even an Isaiah cannot do more than take us into the outer
sanctuary. Of what he felt as he went out to his strange and
dreadful ministry he has not told us, perhaps could not. But
always the question rises insistently, How could a man go
forth to deliver a message, not of warning as if his hearers
might repent and so avert the disaster of which he speaks, but
a message of an irrevocable doom, one in which his own people
were involved? What was it that could sustain him in so harsh
and forbidding a ministry? To ask the question is to be met
with apparent paradox. On the one hand, there can be no
doubt that these men felt deeply the ties that bound them to
their fellows. They loved their country. They were genuine
patriots. Israel's true greatness claimed their devotion. All
that past in which a people rejoices glowed for them with
unique splendor. Amos', "You only have I known of all the
families of the earth"; Hosea's, "I taught Ephraim to walk";
Isaiah's, "I have nourished and brought up children"; all
alike give unmistakable expression to their sense of the tragic
significance of the present situation. Or again, the prayer
upon the lips of Amos, "O Lord, forgive. How shall Jacob
stand, for he is small?" and the refrain with which he represents God as pleading with his people through all the disasters
that had befallen them, "Yet ye returned not unto me"
(4:6ff.), speak eloquently of the prophet's love for his nation.
There is a world of pathos in Isaiah's cry, "Lord, how long?"
as he receives his dread commission. The pain and anguish
that Hosea and Jeremiah felt is reflected in many a heart-

breaking utterance. It was no fantasy playing upon sadistic desire that led these prophets to proclaim destruction.

On the other hand, in their delivering of their message there is infinitely more than a reluctant acquiescence. There is an identification of themselves with their message that reveals itself in the tone of their utterance. Take, for example, Isaiah's announcement of the coming of the day of the Lord:

> Yahweh of hosts hath a day
> Upon all that is proud and haughty . . .
> Upon all the cedars of Lebanon,
> Upon all the oaks of Bashan,
> Upon all the high mountains,
> Upon all hills that are lifted up,
> Upon every lofty tower,
> Upon every fortified wall,
> Upon all the Tarshish ships,
> Upon all pleasant imagery.
> And the loftiness of men shall be bowed down,
> The haughtiness of men brought low;
> And Yahweh alone shall be exalted. (2:12-17)

There is a marvelous lift in the language, a ringing note of exultation. The prophet sees the tempest sweep over the length and breadth of the land, leveling all before it in monotonous ruin and over the desolation shines at last a splendor that is not of this world. It is like the cry of the psalmist set against the background of the storm, "In his temple everything is saying, Glory" (Psalm 29:9). The prophet is at one with himself because he is at one with the will of the God whose majesty he proclaims. A like integration of his being speaks through the passionate invective of an Amos or a Micah. Hosea can forget his own sorrow in the infinitely greater anguish in the heart of God. Jeremiah's keenly sensitive soul can set forth the awful grandeur of an empty world in such a poem as this:

> I beheld the earth, it was waste and void;
> The heavens they had no light.

I beheld the mountains and they trembled,
And all the hills swayed to and fro.
I beheld and, lo, there was not a soul,
All the birds of heaven were fled.
I beheld and, lo, the fruitful land a wilderness,
All the cities thereof were broken down. (4:23-26)

Or again, the prophet's heart can rest in the poignancy of a dirge:

Death is come up by our windows,
It is entered into our palaces,
Cutting off the children from the streets,
Young men from the village square.
And there fall dead bodies of men
On the open field,
As the handful after the harvestman;
But there is none to gather them. (9:21-22)

Joyous youth must untimely die, and the prophet sounds, in that drear fact, the very depths of sorrow and transmutes it into poignant beauty. In poems like these is revealed the wonderful integration of their lives in their intense awareness of God, and of the world as subject to God's sovereign sway. They looked into the face of tragedy and saw life at its darkest, and yet could rest upon the power, the majesty, the righteousness, the holy love of the living God.

"They lived noble lives supported solely by the thought of the unique reality of God," said Cheyne. The thought of God is hardly an adequate phrase. It was the pervading sense of his presence and might that claimed their whole being. As Israel of old, they had been drawn out of themselves into union with overwhelming power; they had made the glad surrender, but for them at the heart of that power was to be found righteousness and truth. And so it was given to them supremely to discern God at work in his world.

It was through their ministry that there came out of the destruction of the nation a new understanding of the holiness of God as the source of the life of the community, that this understanding, infinitely greater than race or blood or soil, holds human beings in a unity most penetrating and intimate, yet provides full scope for the unfolding of the individual life and of that community life in which the present is so deeply involved. Obviously, the message of the prophets for our times is to be found as much in what they were as men as in what they said. We dare not, to be sure, claim for ourselves the pre-eminence which was theirs in the crises of their people's history. "No man taketh this ministry upon himself." But ours may be like theirs, a great certainty that God is now at work in his world, and that, not simply in the ways in which we humbly, gratefully, discern his grace in our lives and the lives of those to whom we minister, but also in the whole of his world, in all its ordered ways—yes, and in its disorder, too, God is at work; even in all the dread destructive energy with which the inhuman mechanization of life is rushing on to its doom, perhaps, though we pray God it may be otherwise, to leave only a heap of ruins behind on which the work of reconstruction will have to begin. If we have eyes to see, we shall discern him in the dread struggle of today, even as an Amos and an Isaiah saw him in the irresistible might of the Assyrian Empire. This empire, as a supreme expression of human pride and arrogance, was ultimately to be overthrown; but, so the prophets declared, it had its part to play in God's great purpose for his world. It has been said with truth that it is not so much world war that is going on as world revolution. Certainly, we cannot shut our eyes to the fact that fundamental changes are taking place in the structural pattern of society. Now revolution "signifieth the removing of those things that are shaken, as of things that are made, that those things that cannot be shaken may remain. Wherefore we receiving a kingdom which cannot be shaken, let us have grace, whereby we may offer service well-pleasing to God with reverence and awe: for our God is a consuming fire" (Heb. 12:27-29). That you will, of course, recognize as New Testament teaching as well

it shall not end yet. By his mere great power on the minds of the now contestants, he could have either *saved* or *destroyed* the Union without a human contest. Yet the contest began. And having begun, he could give the final victory to either side any day.

And thirdly, in a letter written to Thurlow Weed, Republican boss of New York, Lincoln's realization of the difficulty of making his faith understood and his final touching note of humility:

I expect it [the Second Inaugural] to wear as well as—perhaps better than—anything I have produced, but I believe it is not immediately popular. Men are not flattered by being shown that there has been a difference between the Almighty and them. To deny it, however, in this case is to deny there is a God governing the world. It is a truth which I thought needed to be told, and as whatever of humiliation there is in it falls most directly on myself, I thought others might afford for me to tell it.

May God help us to be as those who can afford to speak because we feel that whatever of humiliation there is in the truth we have to declare falls directly upon ourselves.

Let us not think for a moment that this insistence upon the divine transcendence has only negative significance. As we have seen, the prophet's flaming denunciation of the easy identification of a self-centered nationalism with the divine will meant that faith in God could survive the destruction of the nation. It made possible that rebuilding of the community life on entirely new lines which could ensure the continuance of God's use of Israel for his purpose. The prophet's awareness of God at work in the very process of destruction meant that he had not left his world to go its own headlong way.

In the great prophecies associated with the unknown prophet of the Exile there is a vehement question which seems to strike an alien note:

Who gave Israel for a spoil,
Jacob to plunderers? (Is. 42:24)

But this apparently harsh reminder is an integral part of the message of consolation. It was no unknown deity that had overwhelmed them, no inexplicable fate against which they must blindly and helplessly struggle. A stricken, broken fragment of a people, they were still in the hands of their own God, who in the dire misfortune that had befallen them had manifested that awful righteousness of which their own prophets had spoken. Therein lay the hope of the future.

> He hath torn and he will heal us;
> He hath smitten, and he will bind us up. (Hos. 6:1)

His judgment is then no simple sentence of condemnation passed upon evil by One who sits upon his throne at far remove from the human scene; it is an entering into the heart of the conflict. So, in the person of the prophet, feeling, as we have seen in the case of a Hosea or a Jeremiah, all the agony of the crisis, God himself is indeed judging but carrying on, too, his work, his strange work of redemption. In a very real sense the prophets thus anticipated the Christ in whom judgment and redemption are so indissolubly linked together; for judgment, the awful revelation of things as they are and of God as he is, is an inevitable part of the process of redemption. And that redemption of human life, it need hardly be said, looks forward, not backward. No more than forgiveness in the case of the individual, can the redemption of society consist in a simple restoration of the status quo. The new relationship to God means the ingress into life of creative energy, transforming the good and transmuting the evil, shaping out of the raw material of the past a new world of untold possibilities. In every one of the books of the prophets there are, as we know, glowing predictions of what the future holds in store. In all these, while there is an awareness of values of the past, the emphasis falls on the way in which that past will be transcended. It is all summed up in the divine affirmation upon the lips of the great prophet of the Exile, "Remember ye not the former things, neither consider the ways of old. Behold I do a new thing." This openness of the future derived ultimately from the ministry of an Amos or an Isaiah as they denounced the popular identification of God with the hopes and aspiration on which human nature bases its own self-satisfied achievement.

They build up Zion with blood, and Jerusalem with iniquity. The heads thereof judge for reward, and the priests thereof teach for hire, and the prophets thereof divine for money: yet will they lean upon the Lord, and say, Is not the Lord among us? none evil can come upon us. Therefore shall Zion for your sake be plowed as a field, and Jerusalem shall become heaps, and the mountain of the house as the high places of the forest.

But in the last days it shall come to pass, that the mountain of the house of the Lord shall be established in the top of the mountains, and it shall be exalted above the hills; and people shall flow unto it. And many nations shall come, and say, Come, and let us go up to the mountain of the Lord, and to the house of the God of Jacob; and he will teach us of his ways, and we will walk in his paths: for the law shall go forth of Zion, and the word of the Lord from Jerusalem. And he shall judge among many people, and rebuke strong nations afar off; and they shall beat their swords into plow-shares, and their spears into pruninghooks: nation shall not lift up a sword against nation, neither shall they learn war any more. But they shall sit every man under his vine and under his fig tree; and none shall make them afraid: for the mouth of the Lord of hosts hath spoken it. (Micah 3:10-12; 4:1-4)

It has been said with much wisdom that it is when men are conscious of a transcendent end which overrates all lesser claims, that the mood exists in which great experiment is possible.

We moderns may know more than generations of old, but we have lost the sense of vast alternatives, magnificent or hateful, lurking in the background and awaiting to overwhelm our safe little traditions. If civilization is to survive, the expansion of understanding is a prime necessity. (Whitehead, *Modes of Thought,* p. 62f.)

Let me repeat. The essence of the prophets' ministry is to be found in their ability to discern God at work in his world, in their ability to see him in the strange destructive energy of the great empires of their day, empires which were yet ultimately to be destroyed; and yet more significant, perhaps, was their realization that in a mysterious way he was manifesting his power in what he asked them to do and say, so that humbly they knew that human life surrendered to God had its deathless meaning. Let me conclude by setting before you two quotations which seem to me to sum up what I have been trying to say. First, the utterance of the not altogether pleasing, but very sturdy and human, Joab on the eve of battle.

Be of good courage, and let us play the men for our people, and for the cities of our God: and the Lord do that which seemeth him good. (II Samuel 10:12)

And then, this passage from the letter of a French soldier in the last war, and there are many French soldiers like him today (and, please God, there will be more).

Let us bring to everything the spirit of courage. Let us in constant prayer give back our destiny into his hands. Let us humbly admit to him our human hopes, striving at every moment to link them to his eternal wisdom.

Let ours be the unshakable faith that God is at work today in his world in ways not unrelated to our human striving, and we shall bring to him our highest hopes and our highest aspirations; we shall give to the realization of these hopes and aspirations all the effort we can command, making every sacrifice that may be asked of us, blood and sweat and tears; and we shall place all aspiration and effort and sacrifice in God's hands to do with them as he will, not for one moment seeking to prescribe the use he is to make of them but confident that in his will resides our peace, peace that is no mere negation of conflict but the unfolding of all the glorious possibilities of human life lived in its true relationship to God.

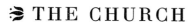 THE CHURCH

ably be considered the goal of human effort. It is, of course, legitimate to follow either method of thought, to begin with unity and ask how the fullest measure of freedom consistent with unity may be reached or to begin with freedom and ask how the fullest measure of unity consistent with freedom may be attained. Both methods have their dangers. A philosophy of emancipation, pure and simple, does not provide much content for life and seems capable of complete realization only by disembodied spirits. The principle of self-determination does not seem likely to prove an adequate solution for all our problems. On the other hand, insistence on unity alone ends in tyranny and fatally inhibits that growth in grace and progress in the knowledge of God to which Christians are called. But assuming that both values are kept full in view, thought would seem truer to life and to history when it begins with unity and proceeds to the consideration of freedom than when it follows the reverse order. Let a man begin with the postulate that he is an entirely separate entity, and his thought cannot escape from the prison house of his own independence. The very power to think at all rests on the primary assumption that man is organic with the universe. The same principle holds true in the field of action. If all men are born free and equal, at least the being born is not a matter of choice. And membership in the family is the given condition in which freedom is to be realized. It may be that at times, for the sake of freedom, the absolute severance of family ties becomes necessary, but this involves serious loss. Ideally, and in normal circumstances, growth in liberty comes within the family life and makes for its enrichment. So it is that liberty attained within unity has larger and wider possibilities than that which is secured by simple sundering of ties. It maintains all its communications while separatism must content itself with freedom within a narrower field. Assigning, then, this primary place to unity as the will of God for man, Catholicism must always insist upon the peculiar gravity of schism as that which violates the fundamental principle of Christian life. It must frankly be acknowledged that insistence upon this truth has in the past too often taken unlovely form. *Corruptio optimi pessima.* Arrogant presumption upon the conviction that "unity" is the first word of religion has been fruitful of the spirit that felt it could go to all lengths in the effort to impose uniformity of belief and practice. As a result, withdrawal from the fellowship for the sake of truth has sometimes seemed practically the only recourse. Hard legalism has blinded men's eyes to the truth that they who cherish unity as sacred must bear the larger part of the responsibility when they force men to sin against it. Time and again it has been forgotten that it is, after all, freedom that gives to unity its deepest meaning. Yet, though all this be granted, in the determinative place given to unity, in the unfaltering insistence on the gravity of schism as striking at the very heart of Christian life, is to be discerned one of the permanent values of the Catholic conception of the Church. If it be objected that this is to make an idol of unity, it may well be answered that this can be true only of the unity of man's devising. The unity that is of God, to which the New Testament bears witness, can hardly be given too profound a reverence.

St. Paul was pre-eminently the apostle of freedom, and of the truth as it is in Christ Jesus; but that which gave its peculiar quality to his work was the determination to realize that freedom and that truth within the unity of the Church, for the sake of the whole Body rather than for the sake of any particular group. The transcendent unity of the Church of God claimed and held his unswerving loyalty. In recent times this has been no more brilliantly set forth than by a Presbyterian scholar, Professor C. Anderson Scott, of Westminster College, Cambridge:

Another name for the *Koinonia* is the Unity. Under this name also Paul traces its existence to the work of the Spirit, and urges the duty of maintaining it (Eph. 4:3). It is the "Unity of the Spirit." In Ephesians 4:13, he indicates its primary sources within the human personality; it is the unity brought about by faith and knowledge of the Son of God. In his eyes it is a sacred thing, and he strives to make those to whom he writes realize its sacredness. When he warns them not to "grieve the Holy Spirit of God," he is really summing up the various precepts which he has just laid down—"lie not one to another"; "be angry and sin not"; "let your speech be not destructive of the moral coherence" but "unto upbuilding." All these find their sanction and appeal in the sense of corporate unity, and in the sacredness of its claim. Whatever denies or injures that corporate unity offends the Spirit who has created, and now maintains, the *Koinonia* (Eph. 4:25-30; cf. Acts 5:3). The same principle is further illustrated by the appearance in the catalogue of "deeds of the flesh" (Gal. 5:19-20) of such things as exhibitions of rivalry, sectarianism, party spirit. Such sins against the body corporate are treated as equally heinous with those against the individual body.

Yet even so eloquent an exponent of the primary place of unity is betrayed, now and again, into utterances which suggest that for him the sense of the whole Church is compounded of lesser unities and is not in itself elemental. He speaks of "the real coalescence of the several groups in which the *Koinonia* was successively embodied. They flowed together spontaneously with the result that there emerged the consciousness of a Catholic *Koinonia*." Is there not here an insufficient recognition of the fact that what effected the intimate unity of the local group was an awareness that the group had been drawn into a larger fellowship? The feel of unity was, doubtless, more vivid within the sphere of its immediate manifestation, but one Spirit of God had called it into being and there was in it from the first, as a significantly creative element, the note of Catholicity. So Harnack, in *Constitution and Law*, has laid it down that "development proceeds in the first place from the whole to the part."

We have had, of late years, all too brief a glimpse of the way in which unity comes. We rejoiced for a season in the laying aside of rivalries and jealousies. Each community realized its own unity as never before. But the temporary unity of the national consciousness was not compounded of these lesser unities. We did not discover ourselves afresh as citizens of New York or Plainville, and then as Americans. It was rather that our new joy in being Americans gave meaning and color to our local affiliations, and these in turn enriched our understanding of what Americanism demanded of us. And beyond Americanism there was a new thrill of world citizenship that for the moment stirred us from our lethargy and was an essential element in our new consciousness of unity. The significant movement was from the whole to the part. It has seemed worth while to labor this truth because so much of our thinking proceeds naturally and rightly in the opposite direction. We begin with our own experience and seek by a process of simple expansion to include the whole within it. And this method has its distinct place and value and its obvious limitations. Not the least of these is the tendency to make us insensitive to the order of life which proceeds from unity to diversity, from God to man first; and then, only then, from man to God. To think of the unity of the primitive Church as the result of synthesis of the several groups is to ignore the part played in invoking the group consciousness by the great creative truth enunciated in St. Paul's reminder to the Corinthians, "To us there is but one God, the Father, of whom are all things, and we in him; and one Lord Jesus Christ, by whom are all things, and we by him" (I Cor. 8:6).

This then is the fundamental truth which the Catholic conception of the Church enshrines. Unity proceeds from above downwards, from within outwards: God's continuous creative act, before it is man's achievement. Thence follows the necessity of the external and visible manifestation of this unity in faith and order. Let thought move prevailingly in the other direction, from the many to the one, and the unity that is attained is merely a logical abstraction, an inner principle to be realized only as differences are laid aside and forgotten. At best they may be tolerated as in some way consistent with a unity that can affect only a part, and that the least distinctive part, of individual lives. The external and visible will, then, be regarded as hindrances to be removed. Religion becomes again an escape from the world. But the establishment of the kingdom of God on earth for which we work and pray means movement earthward, not away from earth. It speaks of unity made visible, not reached by way of abstraction from the outward, but more and more inclusive of the external, making it always the more perfect vehicle of its power. God is seen to be using the outward forms of language, dogma, art, organization, to reveal himself to man. These are not simply touched with a transitory glory. They are not merely concessions to man's weakness. Though derived and secondary, they have permanent and enduring worth because through them God himself draws near to man. Of this sacramental quality the creeds partake. In and through them God declares his truth. Obviously, the creeds cannot be thus considered if we think of them as lifeless documents. They lose nearly all their meaning when treated as the mere subject of antiquarian research. The suggestion made of late that they should be relegated to the back of the Prayer Book as interesting monuments of a dead past is to strip them of their value. The creeds have permanent and enduring worth as they are used and interpreted by the living tradition of the Church, as they awaken a response in countless souls, even as they evoke the honest and sincere questions through which God leads men into deeper understanding of his truth. They are the corporate witness to the unity of the Church's faith. Rightly understood, they do not hamper thought. They indicate the lines along which it may find its truest freedom. They keep before us the proportion of the faith. They remind us constantly that the primary thing is not the emotional state of our inner consciousness but the divine activity, to which our feeling is the response. To urge that creedal expression practically ceased with the fourth century is simply to remind ourselves that we have not kept the unity effected by the Spirit of God. To suggest that we should go behind the creeds to lay the foundation for further formulation of the truth is practically to deny the worth of history. They who believe that through the chaos and confusion of Reformation days God brought to light enduring truth cannot refuse to recognize a like activity of the Spirit in the great formative centuries of the Church's life.

We have named the word "tradition," and we recognize at once that reverence for tradition is one of the characteristics of the Catholic conception of the Church. Naturally, we are tempted to think of the way in which appeal to the past has been so often used to stifle the present. And, indeed, simple appeal to the past as past is a very deadening thing. It is the past as pressing upon the present, and thrusting forward into the future, that must command reverence. Tradition thus conceived is living, massive, and authoritative, though its judgment be pronounced but slowly. It sifts and weighs our guesses and conjectures, our generalizations from our own experience, rejecting this and assimilating that, representing always the wholeness of the Christian faith as over against our partial appropriations of the truth. We may seek to ignore it and our thought will then be impoverished; self-conscious in the degree that we succeed; but even then, it will have its way with us, gathering in whatsoever of truth it may have been ours to glean or burying in decent silence our mistakes. To separate ourselves from it, for the sake of the truth God gives us to see, is to forfeit the opportunity for serving it to the full measure of our ability. There is a passage in the Preface to *Shaking of the Foundations* which may be fairly held to represent the Catholic temper of mind:

What we have written is put forward not as the solution, but as a contribution towards the solution, of the problems we have approached; not as a last word even for our own generation or our own immediate circle but as a word that has come to us and one which we believe we ought to speak. Whatever in it is of value will be absorbed into the common heritage of Christian thought; whatever is crude, misleading, or erroneous will be soon forgotten.

It is in the subordination of the individual to the life of the whole—a subordination which, nonetheless, gives new worth to the individual—that permanent value resides. We are glad servants of the truth rather than its masters. We are reminded always that the unity of the faith is not primarily the unity of our discovery but the unity of God's revelation of himself.

But in the Catholic conception of the Church unity does not only break through human language and claim its determining place in the world of human thinking, ordering diversity into a rich harmony. It invades the sphere of the non-rational and expresses itself in organization. Here again, much depends on the order of our thinking. If unity be only the end to be reached by our effort and organization, a means to that end to be discarded as soon as the end is reached, organization may well be regarded as of only temporary significance. If, however, unity be given in Christ, and it is ours to recognize it and realize it in the terms of our human living, then the organization in which it finds expression will partake of its holiness and have enduring worth as its outward and visible manifestation. Let us admit, for the sake of argument, Professor Scott's contention that in primitive Christianity "the connective tissue which held this larger fellowship together was still *agape* or love"—though this seems to ignore one of the apostolic functions. Is it not of the very essence of Love to desire to express itself in outward and visible form? It cannot remain content with vague aspiration. It will embody itself with word and deed. And is not its hardest task and supreme achievement to be found not in its ability to give utterance and form to moments of intense feeling, but in its ordering and subduing to its own purpose the prosaic humdrum routine of life, making even organization the vehicle of its power to draw men's hearts out of solitude? Being personal, what shall it better use for this purpose than persons, and shall not those who are thus used be recognized as endowed with grace from on high for the particular purpose for which Love seeks to use them? In principle we all acknowledge this. The claim for recognition of every ministry as divinely commissioned is one of the hopeful signs of the progress we are making towards reunion. If the power of God is clearly seen in all that expresses and maintains our lesser unities, we shall not long delay discerning its distinctive manifestations in those through whom the unity of the whole fellowship is expressed and maintained. It is not a simple matter of recognition all round, where the word "recognition" is a blank check to be filled in as every man will, a vaguely generalized term almost emptied of meaning. We need that insight into minute particulars which shall enable us to discern the diversities of gifts, differences of administrations, diversities of operations, in which the divine Love delights to serve. The essential thing is the recognition that the ministry is of God, endowed with his grace for the fulfilment of its tasks. Here, too, we must acknowledge, first of all, the self-same Spirit dividing to every man severally as he will, while we remember that God is a God of order who does not reverse himself, so that his love may be depended upon not to empty old values of meaning as it discovers new values to our sight.

It is hardly necessary to say in conclusion that no one can hope to set forth all the permanent values in the Catholic conception of the Church. Those values are as various as the values of life itself. It has seemed best to insist on one fundamental principle, the way in which thought moves from God to man. Unity is given first and diversity found within us; the wholeness of the revelation in Christ Jesus, and then the freedom wherewith he makes us free; the Spirit that will claim the fulness of God's earth for the manifestations of his glory so that the very substance of its material fabric is transmitted as God seeks to sum up all things in Christ. Unity of faith and order, of sacramental life, these are God's gifts to man in his Church. And worship is its native air because God is above all and through all and in all.

❧ Erasmus: An Evangelical Catholic

Erasmus was a man whose laughter shook the world. In two books which had for that day and age an amazing circulation, *Praise of Folly* and *Colloquies,* he held up to ridicule the ignorance and credulity of priest and friar. His raillery spared neither prince nor prelate nor pope, as he exposed the follies and the frauds of those who professed to serve the Church and the cause of Christ's religion but, in reality, were seeking only their own advantage and profit. And this mockery moved the heart and the conscience of his age because behind the laughter lay a great seriousness. It was this same man who took the lead in bringing the actual text of Holy Scripture within the reach of the plain man, because of his profound faith that the world of his day needed above all a new knowledge of the Christ of the New Testament record. Erasmus, both by his trenchant wit and by the range and grasp of his scholarship, was one of the significant forces that prepared the way for the Reformation. And then, when the issue was fairly joined and the great disruption was in the making, he refused to align himself with those who seemed to be most clearly advocating the reforms to which his own writings had so insistently pointed; and at last he was found in active opposition to the Protestant leaders. He lived and died a Cathoolic. Was this due to timidity or, to put it more kindly, to the reserve of the scholar bewildered by the brutal realities of conflict? Or was he, as some have said more harshly and did say in his own day, just a trimmer, bent on not committing himself until he could triumphantly throw the weight of his learning on the winning side?

It must be admitted that he was thin-skinned and abnormally sensitive to criticism and that his ill health often made him seem unduly preoccupied with his own welfare, but this does but throw into more striking relief the courage and forthrightness with which he set forth his convictions in letters written in profusion both to Reformers and to stalwart defenders of the Catholic cause. His love of truth and his desire to commend it, not unmoved with the very human desire to commend himself, led him to make the most of what he felt to be good and right in the position of those whom he was addressing, but at the same time in almost every instance the note of admonition and of criticism is sounded with unmistakable clearness.

So, writing to Adrian VI, he justly acknowledges that well-meaning Pope's desire to meet the crisis with gentle wisdom rather than with severity; but he goes on in words of solemn warning:

If each is intent on his own private advantage, if theologians demand that on every side their authority shall be bolstered up, if monks allow nothing to be taken away from their privileges, if princes keep a bulldog grip on their every right, it will be very difficult indeed to act for the common good.

In even more emphatic terms than these he had for years been writing to the representatives of powerful vested interests, princes, prelates, inquisitors, urging upon them the grave necessity of reform. He did this, in the words of Emerton, his by no means uncritical biographer, "out of some impelling sense of duty and of right. If we may put any confidence in anything he ever said or did we may rely upon this, that he felt himself the spokesman of a cause greater than himself—the cause of a free and sane scholarship." It was as the servant of truth that for years he did his utmost to secure for Luther a fair hearing. He was convinced that the Reformer had something to say to which the Church ought to give heed; and even after he had come to feel that the dogmatic violence of the Evangelical leaders had put them in the wrong, he for a long time declined to publish anything against them lest he should seem to identify himself with those who sought to check the movement by the exercise of sheer force, by recourse to excommunication, imprisonment, torture, and the stake.

He strikes exactly the same note in his dealings with the leaders on the other side. These sentences from his first letter to Martin Luther are entirely characteristic:

It is better to use in debate reasons which are strong and convincing rather than mere assertions. . . . We must be on our guard against saying or doing anything that savors of arrogance or partisanship. . . . We must keep our minds from being corrupted by anger, hatred, or vainglory for these things too often lie hidden in the very heart of piety.

And in his last letter to the great Protestant leader, when the breach between them was about to become final, Erasmus has this to say:

What you call my weakness or my ignorance is partly conscience, partly the use of judgment. In reading your works, I greatly fear that by some trick Satan is deluding your mind while other things of yours so win me that I want my fears to be false. I am unwilling to profess that of which I am not yet persuaded, much less that which I do not understand.

There is a ring of sincerity about this appeal to conscience and reason that reveals, beyond anything else, the temper of the man. He will not sin against the light. Because of this he has been called the father of modern rationalism. But this is to forget that Erasmus' faith in reason was an integral part of his faith in God. For him God had both revealed himself to man and had endowed man with reason wherewith to understand the revelation. The revelation had been given supremely in the life of Jesus Christ but also in the lives of the saints, in the unwearied efforts of the great theologians to interpret the Gospel in the language of their own day, in the living tradition of the Church.

It is highly significant that along with his devoted labors on the text of the New Testament went his editing of the Fathers, Irenaeus, Cyprian, Athanasius, Chrysostom, Jerome, and Augustine. In these great teachers of the early Christian centuries Erasmus found a breadth and depth of understanding which brought men face to face with life's deepest realities and set its indelible mark on his faith.

In his own day, on the one side, were those in whom reason had broken away from the facts, from the given, the actual, to indulge in mere cobweb-spinning, and for them the refinements and subtleties of the later stages of scholasticism were too often of equal value with the great truths of religion rooted in the experience of the ages. On the other side were those who, feeling intensely the exceeding worth of some part of Christian truth, proceeded to build upon this fragment by a remorseless logic a systematic theology which claimed its own infallibility. From both alike, Erasmus appeals to the wholeness of the divine revelation.

The unity of all truth as deriving from the oneness of God was the cardinal point of his teaching. As a young man, he had written to a friend, "I desire nothing except to secure leisure to live with the whole of my being to the one God." This ardent faith in the unity of God was at the root of his scholarship. It led him to insist that in the heritage of classical antiquity, in all that the Greek mind had contributed to human progress by its relentless questioning, by its concern with intellectual sanity, with balance and proportion, with beauty, the one God had been at work bringing men to a truer appre-

ciation of life's splendor. And for him it was part of the greatness of the Church that it had appropriated so much of this
splendid cultural tradition of the past and made it in no small
degree the vehicle of the Christian message.

It has been said recently that "it is doubtful whether justice
can be done to Erasmus as long as the traditional views of
Protestant and Catholic remain alternatives." This is true if
it means that Erasmus' Catholicism had a breadth and a gen-
erosity, a genuine universality of which as yet this day has
caught hardly more than a glimpse. But it must never be
forgotten that for him these wonderful possibilities of freedom
rest on a profound sense of all that membership in the Body
of Christ means. "I find no fault with liberty that is founded
upon love," (*Libertatem non improbo charitate conditam*),
was one of his sayings—love of God, love of the brotherhood.

For Erasmus was Catholic by every conviction of his being
—Catholic in his refusal to be content with anything less than
the whole range of Christian truth as the stimulus and the
corrective of his own individual thinking; Catholic in his humanism, his belief in the worth and value of the human and
the natural, marred though it may be by man's sin and frailty;
Catholic in his recognition of God at work in the whole of his
universe, and in his consequent refusal to departmentalize
religion and set it over against culture; Catholic in his realism,
in his placing facts before theory, life before logic; Catholic,
above all, in his sense of the unity of the Church, his hatred
of schism, his devotion to a fellowship "whose comprehensive-
ness and continuity are its strength," within which all men
shall think and speak honestly and freely because they love
not their own souls but the God of all truth, whom to serve
is perfect freedom.

OBITER DICTA

❧ On Bremond

In his lively and charming Leslie Stephen Lecture, "The Name and Nature of Poetry," A. E. Housman asks, "Is there such a thing as pure unmingled poetry, poetry independent of meaning?" The question is by no means a rhetorical one, but is to be taken in all seriousness; and the lecturer's own approach to an answer is indicated by his choice of William Blake as the most poetical of all poets, and this on the ground that again and again he "gives us poetry neat or adulterated with so little meaning that nothing except poetic emotion is perceived or matters."

The author of *A Shropshire Lad* thus touches upon a subject which in recent years has been much debated in the realm of literary criticism. In France the controversy was launched by the Abbé Henri Bremond, whose death in August, 1933, brought to the religious world anew a realization of its indebtedness to one who had given to the service of the great Christian tradition a mind exquisitely sensitive to the claims of literature. His monumental *Histoire litteraire du sentiment religieux en France,* now happily in process of translation into English, is distinguished alike for its profound religious perceptiveness and its delicate and subtle appreciation of the harmonies of prose and poetry. It was in 1925 that the sometime Jesuit who had become a member of the French Academy delivered a lecture, entitled *La Poésie Pure.* His thesis ran as follows: "Every poem owes its distinctively poetic character

to the presence, the radiance, the transforming and unifying
activity of a mysterious reality which we call pure poetry."
This is often given in a few lines or even in a phrase which
suffices to stir something in us, to put us in a state of grace
poetically, so that we seek to linger and enjoy, where in prose
we move impatiently on, intent upon the meaning. In poetry,
meaning, logical sequence of ideas, story, detailed description,
are so much impure admixture marring the perfection of the
poetic experience. If it be urged that it is the music of the
language which has this strange power, it may be admitted
that this affords partial explanation, but it cannot account for
the distinction between the verbal music of prose and that of
poetry. Bossuet's prose, he urged, has its own rich organ
notes, but these serve only to reinforce the persuasive power
of his eloquence and do not charm the reader into rapt amaze
as the music of poetry does. Keats' account of the creative
mood seemed to him most suggestive, "an awful warmth about
my heart like a load of immortality"; and he brought his lecture to a climax by adapting a saying of Walter Pater, "all the
arts aspire to the condition of music." "No," said the Abbé,
"all the arts aspire, each by its own proper magical medium—
words, notes, colors, lines—they all aspire to the condition of
prayer."

The lecture provoked an interesting debate in the French
literary reviews, and in defense of his position Bremond did
not shrink from any of the consequences of his theory. "To
accept or even to bring about the silencing of the interior
voices or, in other words, to choke inspiration, is a horrible
thing; but to acquiesce in not translating this inspiration into
verse is the finest homage one can render poetry. The more
one is a poet, the more easily one resists the temptation to
write verse, because the greater one's horror of all poetic expression which of necessity brings in its train, ideas, images,
sentiments." And again, "pure poetry is silence like mysticism. The poet keeps silence or at least inclines to silence,

because the deadly precision of the human word attenuates, disfigures, limits and degrades that mysterious reality which inspiration has allowed him to see, to feel, and almost to touch." The English scholar and poet, and the French savant are, then, in substantial agreement upon this point though, sceptic and priest, they come to it from very different backgrounds.

The Abbé's thought is dominated by his concern for religion. "Pure poetry is silence like mysticism." "The arts all aspire to the condition of prayer." These sentences lie at the heart of his interest in the whole subject and it was not surprising that he presently published a small but significant volume, *Prayer and Poetry* (*Prière et poesie*), in which he explored the affinity between the inspiration of the poet and mystical experience. He began with a rapid review of the history of literary criticism, notable for its judicious selection and masterly discernment of principles. Inevitably and rightly he threw into sharp relief the contrast between the blind rationalism of the eighteenth century and the new insight of the Romantic movement. What he sought to show, and had no difficulty in showing, is that both in the thought of the poets themselves and in the more discerning aesthetic criticism, there is the inevitable recognition of a something beyond reason which, as it has the power to enrich and unify the poet's experience, also enables him to bring his readers to a participation in that experience. A long quotation from Matthew Arnold stood him in good stead. In his essay on Maurice de Guerin that great critic forgets his didacticism to describe the power of poetry as it puts the reader in contact with the essential nature of things, so that he is no longer bewildered and oppressed by them but seizes their secret and is in harmony with them. And it seems altogether fitting that English testimony should be invoked, for the theory of inspiration for which the French writer is contending is almost a commonplace of the English literary tradition. For Wordsworth, as

we know, poetry was "the breath and finer spirit of all knowledge," "the impassioned expression which is in the countenance of all science." Or, to take an American example,
Charles Eliot Norton, in his last lecture at Harvard, spoke of
poetry as a spirit that exists not only in literature, but in art,
in music, in human activity, and doubtless in the whole of life
—something almost the same as beauty itself, that magical
presence which a man from time to time feels surrounding him
everywhere, not quite out of sight, not quite out of earshot,
but for the most part unheard and unseen amid the roar of
the world and the grinding of his own egotism.

Bremond's specific contribution lay in his calling attention
to the way in which poetic sensibility resembles mystical experience. Just as inspiration, in itself indefinable, quickens
and illuminates mind and heart and will, by affording contact
with a larger life, so the mystical ecstasy involves communion
with a reality not to be apprehended by any purely intellectual process, but out of this communion comes in Tauler's
phrase "a distinct, more luminous, more perfect knowledge
of things." Out of his wide reading in literature and mysticism he provides many illustrations of this affinity and indeed
once it is pointed out, a literary critic like John Middleton
Murry seems justified in his surprise that more use has not
been made of the corroboration of religious by poetic experience.

Yet grateful as Christian thought may well be for this fundamental thesis and the skill with which it is maintained, the
book is not without the weakness that attends every effort to
base arguments for religion upon an appeal to the irrational.
In fact, Bremond proves to be seriously affected by the theory of pure poetry to which he had committed himself in the
heat of controversy. To be sure, the term "pure poetry"
hardly appears, save in a footnote where he admits that it is
only an abstraction, but actually the idea haunts him throughout his argument. It is not his exaltation of the unique and

indescribable essence of poetry that is at fault, for in this he may be matched by many Engish writers. They, however, remain aware of the note of rhapsody in their utterances. They do not, as Bremond, attempt to isolate the ineffable and then make this unknown the ground of logical deduction. His scorn of expression because it limits and degrades the mysterious reality of poetic experience, his conviction that in the end to translate inspiration into verse is to do it violence, really make themselves felt in all his treatment of both poetry and prayer. For it is one thing by the use of all one's power of thought to come into the presence of that which is beyond thought; it is quite another to use this something more to cast contempt on the very process of thought by which it has been recognized. Yet that is what the Abbé does in effect when he isolates the moment of ecstatic vision and treats it with its suspension of all the ordinary faculties as an end in itself, as if its very untranslatableness guaranteed its supreme worth. A chapter on the necessary collaboration of *Animus* and *Anima* does, indeed, attempt to restore the balance. The terms are those used in a parable by the distinguished poet Paul Claudel. *Animus* represents the surface self, rational knowledge; *Anima,* the deep self, mystical or poetic knowledge. A long and valuable note insists on the essential and constant solidarity which binds together these two kinds of knowledge. Yet the suggestion remains that they are mutually exclusive, and obviously the descent to particulars is thought of as a falling away from the higher state of communion with reality. But surely the poet's ability to find the inevitable phrases which can communicate his experience can be only arbitrarily distinguished from his power of vision. It is the glory of poetic achievement that words, far from limiting or degrading the poet's sense of life's mysterious depth, enable him to transmit to others what he has seen and felt. In his recent studies in aesthetics Professor S. A. Alexander has been insisting on the importance of the materials with which the artist works, whether stone or pigment, or words, or sounds; so that often in the "feel" of his material he finds a further source of inspiration. It may even fairly be argued that in finding language the poet is himself empowered to discover the deeper meaning of his own experience. The famous opening line of *Endymion,* which Bremond quotes, offers an illustration. If, as seems likely, Keats wrote in the first instance, "a thing of beauty is a constant joy," the plump finality of the concluding phrase would indicate that he had not as yet felt to the full the dynamic eternity of beauty. When the line was made to read, "a thing of beauty is a joy for ever," the liquid flow of the final syllables reveals the poet's new awareness of beauty's living and unfailing power. The phrase has helped him to understand. The moment of vision and the moment of expression are one, almost indistinguishable.

The Abbé recognizes the miracle involved in the endowment of words with the capacity to communicate ecstasy, but he seems to place it on a lower level than what he calls the "higher poetic state." No doubt, he thus discriminates, because human effort plays so large a part in the shaping of verse, whereas the essential poetic experience like that of the mystic seems to come entirely of itself, and its givenness is taken as a sign of its superior value. It would, indeed, be ill to deny the presence of this mysterious factor, or to fail to recognize its complete otherness from anything that can be attained by deliberate effort alone, but there is grave danger of forgetting that the great moments come only to minds prepared and that the disciplined effort which precedes vision or follows it for the sake of conveying it to others, partakes also of divine grace. Wordsworth is to the point when he speaks of "the vision and the *faculty* divine."

"The source of inspiration" says Bremond, "can be reached by no manner of reflection." True enough, but is it ever reached, can it be reached, by those who do not reflect? We are obviously here engaged in the familiar discussion of the respective merits of rational and intuitive knowledge, a discussion which must always end in the discovery that each is indispensable to the other. It may be worth recalling a passage in Coleridge's *Biographia Literaria,* in which the relationship between the two is splendidly put. He is speaking of the way in which Shakespeare achieved in the writing of his plays, a reconciliation between creative power and intellectual energy. "What then shall we say? Even this; that Shakespeare, no mere child of nature; no automation of genius; no passive vehicle of inspiration possessed by the spirit, not possessing it; first studied patiently, meditated deeply, understood minutely, till knowledge become habitual and intuitive, wedded itself to his habitual feelings, and at length gave birth to that stupendous power."

Again, Bremond's isolation and exaltation of the moment of apprehension, whether mystical or poetical, at the expense of its context disparages the will and the emotions, as well as the intellectual faculty. It looks in the direction of that passivity which has always haunted the mystical tradition. There is, indeed, a chapter, "The Specific Activity of the Mystics," which recognizes the danger of the emphasis upon passive states and insists that along with the suspension or paralysis of the ordinary faculties, there is a redoubling of the deeper activities of the soul as it dilates itself to take the divine gift into the inmost recesses of its being. But it is to be noted that his activity is one which is directed entirely away from earth and the human scene, and is, in fact, only a kind of receptivity. So, in the final chapter, it is asserted that "the poet in the last resort is but an evanescent mystic whose mysticism breaks down." Breaks down, because he turns back to the world in the effort to communicate his message. In other words, he forsakes pure poetry. This is his infirmity; poetic inspiration with its desire to share the vision, moves on a lower level than that mystical experience in which the soul is wholly absorbed in the act of uniting itself with reality. "The inspiration" he says explicitly, "is in the original movement and not in the course of action which follows it. . . . In that delicious numbness of which we have just heard and not in the labor which is going to follow." No doubt, the note of detachment is an indispensable element of the mystical experience, an element all too easily overlooked in these days of bustling activity; but to take it for the whole, to treat it as the supreme climax to the exclusion of everything else, leads all too easily to a morbid quietism. It is worth remembering that quietism has always tended to neglect and even to despise vocal prayer.

It is because this tendency reveals itself in Bremond that it seems fair to speak of the essential passivity involved in his conception of poetry and prayer, and confirmation for this is to be found in his treatment of Aristotle's concept of catharsis. Confessedly this is a very thorny subject. There has been endless discussion of the great sentence: "Tragedy then is an imitation of an action that is serious, complete, and of a certain magnitude . . . through pity and fear effecting the purgation of such emotions." Evidently "the purgation (catharsis) of such emotions" is the crucial phrase. Bremond makes play with some of the fanciful interpretations of French classical criticism, and then for his part contends that purging means "purging away." "The catharsis purges us of all pity, of all fear, of all love," and must do this because "the passions obstruct the activity of the deeper soul." In this he is again controlled by his conviction that to feel deeply is a falling away from that emotionless communion with reality, which is the *summum bonum*. But the truer interpretation is surely that which thinks of the cleansing of the emotions. In the presence of great tragedy, the spectator, face to face with suffering far greater than his own can ever be, is lifted out of himself into the great stream of life. What is purely personal and self-regarding drops away. Fear becomes a deep sense of awe before life's mystery; as the taint of egoism is removed, pity loses its note of superiority and is changed into love. They who are thus moved do not feel less but more in that moment of understanding, for they are one with all mankind. The Abbé's failure to see this was the result of his preoccupation with the soul's movement away from the here and now. The logic of his position would lead him on to what Hocking calls "a world-avoiding, illusion-casting, zero-worshipping mysticism." What is wanting is the discriminating balance of von Hügel's account of the mystical state. "The active and the contemplative life are ultimately but two mutually complementary sides of life so that no life ever quite succeeds in eliminating either element; and life, *ceteris paribus,* is complete and perfect as it embraces both elements each at its fullest and the two in perfect interaction; the Negative Abstractive way peremptorily requires also the other, the Affirmative Concrete way." This is worlds away from the ideal of a passionless soul in the embrace of a passionless God, which Bremond's thought would seem to set before us.

For in the end this passivity strangely infects the conception of ultimate being. Reality would seem to lie inert in the background until, as it were, stimulated into some sort of response by the seeking soul, which in turn becomes merely receptive. There is little or no feeling for the way in which reality comes to meet us. God himself is immobilized. Probably von Hügel has this in mind when, in speaking of the one-sided character of Neo-Platonism, he notes its incapacity to find any descending movement of the Divine into human life. It is just this movement of God earthward that we are now learning to take seriously. Whitehead's insistence on the creative passage of nature gives new meaning to the scholastic statement that God is One, *Actus Purus,* Sheer Energy. Truth, beauty, goodness, are no remote abstractions; they are the ways in which the divine energy breaks in upon human life. The will of God to create and to redeem is in ceaseless operation. The quickening, light-producing effect of inspiration, the strange capacity for endowing words with new power, are not indications that for the poet contact with reality has been broken as he turns towards his fellowmen. Rather he has become the vehicle through which reality is revealing itself. Consider again the Abbé's account of the three phases of the poetic experience as a whole: "A dull and painful gestation of mind or heart with tumultuous useless attempts at invention or decision; then comes the spark of inspiration; and then a joyful fertility of the mind, or a gay decision of the heart." His further statement that the first and last phases contain nothing but the more or less intense exercise of our ordinary faculties, may be disregarded and attention fastened instead on the relation between the three phases. The depth and richness of the great moment of simplification are in proportion to the vigor and sincerity of the thinking that has gone into the time of preparation, just as the same depth and richness are fully known only as the labor of expression is marked by a like sincerity, and the poet is not disobedient to the heavenly vision. Is it not in the process as a whole that the true analogue of prayer is to be found? It has its origin in a confused welter of longings and desires. Its first effort must be to bring order out of chaos, for true prayer is the expression of our whole being not simply of our surface wishes. It is the soul's sincere desire unuttered or expressed. It is only as the struggle to know our own will is honest and persistent, that we have anything to offer for union with the divine will. The moment of apprehension that God gives discovers to us the deeps of our own being as it unifies our desires, purging them of selfishness and giving them creative power. This has obvious affinity with the enriching simplification that comes to the poet. There follows then the translation into deed and word of this new understanding of the will of God and our own desire, the return upon life with enhanced perception and energy. Through every stage an Other-than-self has been cooperating. In the first promptings and strivings God is at work as surely as he is in the moment of apprehension, and must be in the task that follows if it is to be fruitful.

Prayer means then no blind surrender to the divine will, even as poetry is no mere absorption in the poetic ecstasy. In that fusion of deepest longing with the purpose of God, all that is sincere and real of individual desire is preserved and made effective. As the poet speaks of ultimate reality with his own unique note of understanding that has its source in the struggle both before and after vision comes, so in prayer personality is unified and deepened through the soul's offering of itself to God, and the effort to know one's own desires and to bring them, enriched and clarified, to bear upon life, plays its very significant part in the process. "The Spirit itself beareth witness with our spirit that we are the sons of God," but each of us must declare his unique sonship with his own individual accents.

> And so the Word had breath and wrought
> With human hands the creed of creeds,
> In loveliness of perfect deeds,
> More strong than all poetic thought.

One might almost dare to make the last line read: "And power of true poetic thought!"; for that life was at once the perfect poem and the perfect prayer.

⋟ On Bergson

It is twenty-five years since *Creative Evolution* appeared, but
many of us still remember the excitement—that is precisely
the word—with which we read that magnificent book. We
had become accustomed to thinking of evolution in the terms
of the redistribution and recombination of given factors, and
the bondage of merely mechanical conceptions was heavy
upon us. The best we could do philosophically was to make
ourselves comfortable in a block universe, using religion or
some form of idealism to adorn and conceal the walls of our
prison house. And suddenly we were once more brought face
to face with the amazing fact of life in its inexhaustible resources. We had begun to think of adaptation to environment
as almost an end in itself until circumstances seemed, as it
were, the rigid mold into which life must be poured and fixed.
Now we came to see it, instead, as simply one of the conditions of life's victory over its surroundings. Variation, which
had seemed so prosaic a matter as long as change was thought
of as slow and gradual, was seen to be a revelation of life's
power to put forth ever new efforts in its onward march. The
very title, *Creative Evolution*, was eloquent. The vital impulse is the will to create.

All living beings hold together and all yield to the same tremendous thrust. The animal takes its stand on the plant, man be-
strides the animal world, and the whole of the human race throughout
space and time is one vast army about us, before us, and behind us,

charging forward dashingly to beat down every resistance and clear every obstacle, perhaps even death itself.

It was language like that that made us actually feel life's creative energy.

Yet, substantial as is the contribution thus made to religious thinking [by *The Two Sources of Religion and Morality*], it must be admitted that doubts and questionings arise not unlike those which followed when the enthusiasm of a first reading of *Creative Evolution* had subsided. In that book, as we have seen, the insistence upon the primacy of intuition involved a rather thoroughgoing disparagement of the intellect. Now to dwell upon the limitations of the intellect is, no doubt, a necessary task, for it is only too ready, like Lucifer, to exalt its throne above the stars of God. Yet granting all the danger that attends abstraction and analysis, the danger of remaining content with a partial or mutilated view of reality, are not these processes a necessary stage in the progress toward truth; and are not the dangers due to the abuse of the method rather than essential to it? If the intellect is a faculty inherently deceptive, it is hard to understand how it could ever have discovered and proclaimed its own defect. It may fairly be asked, too, whether there is not a latent dualism in Bergson's thought. On the one hand is life, durée, energy, movement, actual experience of flux and variety; on the other is matter, space, arrest, fixity. It is only with these latter that, in Bergson's account, logical and conceptual thinking has to do, and the terms applied to them are generally degradation and descent. It is always difficult for one who has his own experience of the supra-rational to recognize the worth of the ordered, lowly ways of human thinking.

Not unlike this is the dualism underlying the present book. The distinction between open and closed morality, and that between dynamic and static religion, is immensely important. It is not new; in fact, it is as old as Isaiah. "Forasmuch as this people draw nigh unto me, and with their mouth and with their lips do honor me, but have removed their heart far from me and their fear of me [that is to say, their religion] is a commandment of men which hath been taught them" (Is. 29:13). But Bergson has, as perhaps no one else, set this distinction before us in all its bearings and associations, and philosophy will be the richer for his ample and subtle elaboration of it. The question is whether in exalting open morality and dynamic religion to its rightful place, he does not unduly depreciate the other types. The very names he gives them, "closed" and "static," betray and convey a certain prejudice. Admittedly they have their very grave limitations and dangers, but are they as inherently negative and obstructive as Bergson would seem to say; or does the difficulty really lie in a tendency of human nature to substitute the means for the end? Our Lord himself was a Jew and wept over Jerusalem. Internationalism that knows nothing of patriotism easily becomes a barren cosmopolitanism.

Religion, too, cannot remain a sheer qualitative flux of emotion. It must embody itself in word and deed. If it is to be communicated it must find appropriate language, forms or words, always inadequate and always likely to be substituted for reality, but nonetheless indispensable. Bergson would, no doubt, admit this. Indeed, he acknowledges the way in which open and closed morality are interfused, each deriving something from the other. Static religion often cherishes and keeps alive the fire of mysticism and is thus the means by which this touches the plain man. But the total impression that the book makes is of a contrast so sharp and clear as to be entirely divisive. His long chapter on "static" religion, with its comprehensive survey of primitive stages, is in some degree vitiated by the failure to see that the myth-making instinct may be in large part a naïve response to the impact of the vital impulse, just as his own wonderful book is in a sense an elaborate and brilliant product of the same instinct.

"Closed" and "static" are sometimes referred to as "natural," and by inference "open" and "dynamic" are supernatural. Once more, the distinction is exceedingly worth while, but we do not want again to set the two in diametrical opposition. The mystic is always in danger of doing that. Bergson suggests as the *two sources of morality and religion:* Nature, or perhaps more specifically the necessities of group life, and God. But, we ask, is not group life also ordained of God? Two modes of derivation perhaps—one mediate, the other immediate; but hardly two sources. It is so great a book that one could wish that it had been given another title.

≥ On Gilson

It is not, of course, to be denied that there are large and indispensable elements of truth in value-theology. The grave defect of Barthianism is its failure to take account of these. But what must always be held fundamental is the absolute priority of God. This means the rejection of any assumption that "prior to God or to God's revelation of himself or man's experience of faith in him, the mind is in possession of a valid standard by means of which it can judge God and his revelation." L. P. Jack's penetrating saying, "God is not so much the object as the source of the will to believe," looks in the same direction. Medieval insistence on the primary significance of Being holds fast to the "givenness" of that which the mind seeks to interpret and in theory at least maintains always the transcendence of God. For as Etienne Gilson writes in *The Spirit of Medieval Philosophy*: "Beyond all sensible images and all conceptual determinations, God affirms himself as the absolute act of Being in its pure actuality."

✶   ✶   ✶

To distinguish between necessary Being and contingent being is no mere play upon words. It is to conserve both sides of a fundamental paradox. On the one hand, everything is dependent at every moment of its existence on the Source of all being: "Thou takest away their breath, they die." In Gilson's more technical language, "As soon as the sensible world is regarded as the result of a creative act, which not only gives it existence but conserves it in existence through all successive moments of its duration, it becomes so utterly dependent as to be struck through with contingency down to the very roots of its being." God penetrates then to the very depths of nature. Not in the first instance the form of things, but the very being of things is from him. On the other hand it is *being* that is conferred, even though it be only derived being, and being involves actuality of self-existence. A created object is more than the shadowy representation of something else, a mere symbol. Paul Tillich among writers of today puts it well: "Creation produces something new which did not exist and which after being produced represents something independent and singular. Our life has this tension between dependence on the origin that has produced us and the independence of it through individuality and freedom." Individuality and freedom are inherent in the being which God confers. It is not strange that the man who is to my mind the ablest exponent of Thomism today, Erich Przywara, quotes with approval this argument from Kierkegaard: God's omnipotence is his goodness. For Goodness is complete giving but in such a way as to make the receiver independent. All finite power makes dependent; only omnipotence can make independent, can bring forth out of nothing that which has being (*Bestand*) in itself. This is the inconceivable thing: that omnipotence can produce not only the most imposing of all things, the totality of the visible world, but also the most fragile of all things; that omnipotence, which can rest upon the world with so mighty a hand, can nonetheless make itself so gentle that that which comes into being receives independence.

It is, perhaps, unorthodox to quote the passage in this connection but the words of the Fourth Gospel, "As the Father hath life in himself so hath he given the Son to have life in himself," do describe the kind of giving of which Omnipotence is capable and may remind us that there is an analogy between the doctrine of the Incarnation and the relation of God to his world. Theories of emanation from deity give only the continuity of God with his world and religiously issue in a pantheistic pietism which dissolves individuality in a mist. On the other hand, theories of a Demiurge who shapes alien material according to a pattern limit severely the scope of the divine activity and leave much in the universe radically independent of God.

❧ On Nietzsche

Zarathustra is the lyrical record of a spiritual struggle, though the writer would vehemently have disclaimed the word "spiritual," the long and tortured struggle of a soul and its triumphant issue. All this is unknown ground to A. H. J. Knight, author of *Some Aspects of the Life and Work of Nietzsche,* and his ignorance leads to grave misunderstanding. *Zarathustra,* forsooth, is "not personal experience, sentiment, prejudice or reminiscence but an astonishing objective creation the fruit of inspiration not reflection." And again, somewhat inconsistently, he maintains that Nietzsche brings the idea [of Eternal Recurrence] forward in the third part of the book, having held it back that it may make the most effective appearance possible, not seeing that, as it stands, it has its due and inevitable place in the record of Nietzsche's experience. More seriously, he spends pages in showing that Nietzsche must have known that the idea of Eternal Recurrence was to be found in Greek philosophy, that he was therefore insincere in claiming to be the first to teach this doctrine, and that if he is insincere once where it does not much matter, it is extremely probable that he will be insincere in other places where it does matter. Whereas, it is the obvious truth that Nietzsche was certainly the first, as probably he will be the only man, to teach Eternal Recurrence as the ultimate mystery of the Universe and an object of adoration. Of the reality and depth of this religious conviction there can be no more striking evidence than a much quoted passage from the last paragraphs of *The Will to Power*. It is that in which he draws a contrast between Dionysus and the Crucified One. "The God on the Cross is a curse upon life" is a sentence which leaves one torn between horror at the blasphemy and grief for the woeful misunderstanding that gave it birth. But it should not blind the eyes to the positive value of the affirmations of the passage. "The problem is that of the meaning of suffering; whether a Christian or a tragic meaning be given to it. In the first case, it is the road to a holy mode of existence; in the second case, *existence itself is regarded as sufficiently holy* to justify an enormous amount of suffering." Too often the preaching of the Cross moves on a *quid pro quo* level and misses the note of essential tragedy and the witness that it bears to the greatness and goodness and the holiness of life, while it forgets that redemption is only possible and conceivable if that already exists which can justify the agony of suffering which redemption costs.

For the consideration of Nietzsche's ethical teaching it is of the first importance to keep in mind this religious background rather than its possible Greek antecedents. There is, of course, a radical inconsistency in urging men to a particular line of conduct when all that they do is rigidly determined by what has been done countless times before; but such inconsistency is not unknown in other forms of religion. And the unsparing denunciation of moral codes has also its counterpart in the antinomianism that so often accompanies fanatical belief. Indeed, there are not wanting signs that now and again Nietzsche felt that there was some sort of affinity between his teaching and that of the Christianity which he treated with such contempt. "The whole psychology of the gospels," he says in *The Antichrist*, "lacks the concept of guilt and punishment as also that of reward." And again, in *Beyond Good and Evil*, "Jesus said to his Jews: 'The law was for servants;—love God as I love him, as his Son! What have we Sons of God to do with morals?' " That his ethical teaching springs out of religious belief neither gives it validity nor condemns it but makes the more imperative a careful discrimination. It is easy and necessary to recognize the unbounded egotism, the strident megalomania which finds so frequent expression in his writings. It is right to ask how far in these his madness casts its shadow before. He may be taken as an example of what religious fanaticism can be at its worst. But those who have felt the passionate sincerity of the man, as for example it is revealed in his letters, will not be content until they have found the positive values which for all their perversion and one-sided exaggeration make him a significant figure in man's spiritual history. It will always be remembered, too, that he has suffered as much from the foolish enthusiasm of his followers as from the uncomprehending hostility of his opponents.

"Live dangerously" is his cry. Dangerous doctrine, indeed; but after all Safety First is not quite the same as the experience of salvation. "More belief in life summons one to work at the future and redeem all that hath been by creating." No doubt, the wild and wilful exaggeration of his utterance gives countenance to those who interpret his Will to Power, the will to create, as the will to be rough. No doubt, the scorn he pours upon the maudlin self-indulgence in the luxury of others' woe, which often passes for pity, may justify those who find in him only contempt for the weak. Yet Dostoevski in his strange pictures of human life in the most abject conditions is singularly free from that pity which would appropriate others' weakness and mold it upon one's own will. His is, after all, that reverence for great misfortune, for great ugliness, for great failure of which Nietzsche speaks. We sometimes forget that those in sorrow may need more than anything else the "unmoved eye and the look of eternity." It is easy, again, to see that preoccupation with the special responsibilities, the heroic undertakings to which the strong are called, may and does in his writings involve a disastrous contempt for the humbler tasks. No one of his catchwords but is full of danger—no one but has been wrested by his followers to their own damnation, as they take from him that which is easy and leave that which is hard. And no one of them but constitutes a challenge to the lethargy of men's souls.

He can hardly be made a doctor of the Christian Church. His blasphemies forbid that; but it is not for us to say whether these are more bound up with his own blindness than with the unreal presentment of Christianity with which he was familiar. He remains a prophet and one who offers an illustration of his own saying, "the great scorners are the great reverers," for "is it not thy piety itself that letteth thee no longer believe in God?"

❧ On D. H. Lawrence

It must frankly be admitted that, pitifully enough for the great majority of people, Lawrence will be known only as the author of a novel which some of them have read and many have not read, but which all will agree is the last word in indecent literature. Any estimate of Lawrence must, therefore, face fairly the fact of this book. It would be useless to attempt to palliate the offence against good taste. The use of ugly four-letter words shatters the unity of the style and from the literary point of view produces an effect far more unpleasant than that given by a like vocabulary in Joyce's *Ulysses,* where the words are in keeping with the characters and the whole of the setting. More serious to many minds is the preoccupation of the book with sexual experience and the detailed descriptions of the act of coition. It is, I confess, difficult to rise to the full height of the author's intention as he seeks to celebrate the phallic mysteries, but, waiving the question of the legitimacy of his purpose, one is bound to admit that there are passages in which the language has just the touch of exaltation, the power of tranfiguring the actual, which befits hierophantic utterance. But these lyrical passages are constantly marred by the intrusion of the bald blunt words that seem deliberately intended to shock the consciousness of the reader and do so because they unawares give expression to that almost brutal contempt for natural functions which in many people is the uglier side of their sense of shame. Lawrence desires to convey an incommunicable mystery. He knows full well that this can only be done on the wings of the imagination. But this mode of utterance will be understood only by the few; and in his desire to make himself clear to a larger circle, he uses the very vocabulary that was, in reality, coined to profane the mystery. There lies the tragedy of the book. In a letter he writes, "Myself I write in all honesty and in the sincere belief that the human consciousness needs badly now to have the doors freely opened into the dark chamber of horrors of sex—it is no chamber of horrors really, of course—and I feel the language needs to be freed of various artificial taboos on words and expressions." But the taboos are not merely artificial. Behind the conventional insistence upon them there lies a deeply rooted instinctive protest againts the life-denying implications of the words. It was, no doubt, his loneliness that made him somewhat oblivious of this. Resentful of anything approaching the coarse humor of the smoking-room story, quick to express his distaste for indecency of any sort, himself withdrawn from most of the ordinary associations with his fellow men, he evidently had no sense of the vulgar contempt for life processes which the common use of these words represents, a contempt which he would have considered a cardinal sin.

It cannot be denied, of course, that he was woefully one-sided, but it is characteristic of a prophet to be one-sided. He feels so intensely one aspect of reality that he cannot wait to get perspective. And it must be remembered that for him sexual experience brought to a focus, as it were, that immediacy of contact with a pervasive life other than one's own, upon which he was convinced that all rich and full living must depend. This contact, however, is made below the level of consciousness and therefore remains a mystery. Hence, his frequent use of the words "dark" and "darkness." It is a nature mysticism fully as much as a sex mysticism. He felt himself driven to give expression to the value and significance of man's relationship to the dark presence that lies beyond the boundaries of the conscious regard. It was a religious task. "There is a *principle* in the universe," he writes to a friend, "towards which man turns religiously—a *life* of the universe itself. And the hero is he who touches and transmits the life of the universe." And again in another letter, and this when in the throes of writing *The Rainbow*: "Primarily I am a passionately religious man, and my novels must be written from the depth of my religious experience." And still earlier, "One needs something to make one's mood deep and sincere. There are so many little frets that prevent our coming at the real naked essence of our vision. It sounds boshy, doesn't it? I often think one ought to be able to pray, before one works—and then leave it to the Lord. Isn't it hard, hard work to come to real grips with one's imagination—throw everything overboard? I always feel as if I stood naked for the fire of Almighty God to go through me—and it's rather an awful feeling. One has to be so terribly religious to be an artist."

This it is which lies behind the passionate sincerity of his writings, whether novels or poems or letters. It is the "terrifying honesty" of a William Blake, with whom he has well been compared. All this John Middleton Murry signally fails to appreciate as he goes on sensing, suspecting, and fearing things in the background. But for those who in the name of the Christian religion desire to take up the long-postponed task of facing fairly the appallingly difficult problem of sex, Lawrence's frankness has provided a vast amount of data with which they will have to reckon. It may help them to remember that he was above all a faithful husband, detesting promiscuity and scornful of all who would trifle with the mystery.

Like all the prophets Lawrence was a very lonely man. He hungered after friendship but could not endure pretense. His

numen, his Holy Ghost, with which Murry makes so scornful play, drove him at times to deal faithfully with his
friends, and they could not understand. He blamed himself in
later life for the repression of his societal impulses. This repression undoubtedly existed and was, in part, one of the effects upon him of the Great War. Murry has enlarged upon
this in his comment in the chapter, entitled "The Nightmare
in Kangaroo," but he does not give sufficient place to its total
impact upon Lawrence, for whom the war revealed the massive
weight of that mechanized materialism which denies the worth
so the individual soul. Lawrence detested it, too, because it
gave vogue to many grandiose phrases which are only substi-
tutes for genuine feeling.

The fact is that Murry is temperamentally quite incapable
of understanding Lawrence. This comes out quite clearly in
the *Letters*. "Don't you think it's nonsense," he writes, "when
Murry says that my world is not the ordinary man's world and
that I am a sort of animal with a sixth sense? Seems to me
more likely he's a sort of animal with only four senses—the
real sense of touch missing. They all seem determined to make
a freak of me—to save their own short-failings, and make
them normal." Apparently, the intense organic sensibility
which made the very feel of things the determining factor in
Lawrence's life was to Murry almost unknown.

❧ On Keats

It is a profoundly interesting study that John Middleton Murry (*Keats and Shakespeare*) has given us of the making of a great soul, and I for one find it convincing. It is a little difficult to follow him in some of his exegesis. I am not sure, for example, that the simple eloquence of the statement, "I have loved the principle of beauty in all things," will bear the philosophic strain that he puts upon it; and I fear that I do not begin to get all out of either the first or the second *Hyperion* that he finds there. As I read again, in Miss Lowell's narrative, the story of those last pitiful days in Italy, I wonder whether Keats had found that complete reconciliation with life which Murry claims for him—his refusal to write to Fanny Brawne or to hear from her seems to me to strike the note of rebellion rather than acceptance. After all deduction for the zeal of the enthusiast, we must admit that the case is clearly made for the inclusion of Keats among the great saints of literature.

I use the word "saint" advisedly, for I hold that Murry is supremely right in his claim that what declares itself in the poet is a form of religious experience. Certainly, it is impossible not to see in the surrender of a man's whole being in warm, rich, loving acceptance of life that offering of one's self, one's soul and body, in self-forgetful adoration, which is of the very essence of worship. The cry of eager triumph,

Thou wast not born for death, immortal Bird!
No hungry generations tread thee down . . .

freely lifts the poet's own sense of mortality into self-less
union with a deathless glory. "Dying and behold we live." In
the familiar lines,

Bold Lover, never, never canst thou kiss,
Though winning near the goal—yet, do not grieve;
She cannot fade, though thou hast not thy bliss,
Forever wilt thou love, and she be fair!

there is the sense both of the joy and the pain of our fleeting
human experience and of the splendor and the tragedy of the
perfection of eternity, and these are all fused in the awe-
struck recognition of the beauty of ultimate reality.

Beauty is truth, truth beauty,—that is all
Ye know on earth, and all ye need to know.

are lines which may be hopelessly vague and inadequate as a
logical account of the universe but are easily intelligible as an
act of worship.

My only criticism of Murry's zealous claim for the recognition of all this as true religion would be that he shuts us up,
as narrowly as any ecclesiastic, to one particular form of experience and even seems to make salvation depend upon artic-
ulateness. Such a position ignores the quiet, heroic faith and
courage with which countless simple souls face life's mystery
and, in the doing of the day's work, feel that they are being
used for a purpose far beyond themselves. They speak in conventional language, for they have no ability to coin phrases of
their own; but that does not mean that they think only by formula or feel only by proxy. They have their own inner life and
in their own way prove axioms upon their pulses and are in
vital touch with reality. In forgetfulness of these Murry seems

unconsciously to be in danger of setting up an orthodoxy of romantic literature which finds delight only in its own shibboleths. Yet, after all, this is but the enthusiasm of the convert and the almost inevitable corollary of his intensity of vision; and we can forgive his narrowness for the sake of the profound sympathy and understanding with which he takes us to the creative center of the poet's life.